Virginia Colonial Abstracts
Vol. #1

LANCASTER COUNTY VIRGINIA

Record Book No. 2

- 1654-1666 -

By:
Beverley Fleet

Southern Historical Press, Inc.
Greenville, South Carolina

Please direct all correspondence and orders to:

www.southernhistoricalpress.com
or
**SOUTHERN HISTORICAL PRESS, Inc.
PO BOX 1267
375 West Broad Street
Greenville, SC 29601
southernhistoricalpress@gmail.com**

ISBN #0-89308-161-2

Printed in the United States of America

Preface.

At best abstracts can be little more than an index. A guide
to the original records. In taking these it was my intention
that they be solely for my own use. As I worked, various persons not only requested references but further suggested that
I release them. However being fully informed that this meant
a certain financial loss, a very limited number of copies have
been prepared.

Students of Virginia genealogy all realize the difficulties
encountered in reading the early Lancaster records. Mr. Stanard
considered them the most trying in all Virginia. Record Book
#2 is not as difficult as the others of the period (see page
461). I trust, however, that students who consult these abstracts
will bear with me and realize that I have followed the original
as closely as I was able to do. There are names in the records
of this county that, to say the least, are uncertain. We also
know only too well that the chief delight of almost every gen-
ealogist is to discover an error made by another. It would
never do to disappoint those who are so much the holier.

In being able to work in the Archives Department in the
State Library in Richmond, all of us owe a debt of gratitude
to Mr. Morgan Robinson. But for this gentleman's careful and
not always appreciated efforts, we would have no place to
work and nothing to work upon. Our historians and genealogists
should be devoutly thankful to him.

In working in the Archives Department, Mrs James Claiborne
Pollard and Miss Estelle Bass have assisted in every way.
These Virginia gentlewomen have been patient and courteous,
not to say witty and delightful, in their help to me while
taking these abstracts. I greatly appreciate their kindliness.

Beverley Fleet.
Box 161. West End Station,
Richmond, Virginia.

Lancaster Co. Va. Record Book #2.
1654-1666.

page 1.

Ho'd Sir
    Services to you & your wife presented These are to let you understand
that I am by Elias Edmonds his last will and testament sole overseer of
his Estate & see that his children be not cheated and defrauded of that
Estate their father left them Yet John Meredith and Walter Heard not giving the Court intelegence thereof as I hear obtained an order for administration of the estate nor I not having any notice thereof saying that
his Mother in Law Mrs Edmonds made no will therefore the Court granted
letters of administration (now I can prove but this Court is so remote
that I cannot bring witnesses) that Mrs Francis Edmonds made a noncupa-
tive will which I know in Law is authentick besides there are great debts
claimed by some namely Mr Meredith out of the Estate per account woh I
know is contrary to the act of Assembly in such cases yet notwithstanding if it be Meridiths right God forbid but he should have it but I can
prove that the great accompt brought in against Elyas his Estate did
nothing appertain to Elyas nor ought not to be paid out of the sd Estate
all which I can prove & shall make appear at the next Court Meredith his
pretense is that I am a Papist and not to have the bringing up of the
children which God knows was none of my intent but that some honest
careful man should breed them up and not diminish the Estate which I am
shure is a good Virginia Estate there is not all incerted in the Inventory
besides the debts ought to be paid before Legacies It was Mr Edmonds
wil & desire that his Estate should not be administered on nor any way
alienated by appraisel therefore I beseech you if it be possible not to
grant Letters of administration until the next Court held for this County
for I conceave the Children to be in a desperate condition if you let the
sd Meridith & Heard proceed in what they desire the Inventory is not yet
proved nor the will therefore good sir if it be possible grant a reference
of all business of that Estate to the next Court held at Ma'r Carters
house where God willing I shall attend you God forbid but the will of
the decd should be performed so near as may be they are to have all the
increase of their cattle both male and female you will say who will keep
the children upon these terms I answer I will find those that shall keep
them and give them better Education than those in whose Custody they are
I have that to show the Court under Mr Edmonds his hand that the Court
doth not know of nor yet concieve Therefore I desire that administration
may be suspended and all business concerning that Estate might to the next
Court that I may be there that hath the whole oversight of the Estate &
no man else I know much concerning the greatest debts that are claimed &
can I hope secure the Estate from paymt of some of them I pray sir for
the good of the fatherless and motherles Children be so charitable as to
stop proceedings and to grant this request to
        Sir Your Obliged friend & servt to use
                                            Edwin Conaway
From my house at the head of Corotoman March the 27 (54)

Postscript
    Sir he hath not put in security nor proved the will as yet therefore
the Court may be pleased to stop the proceedings All the tobacco belonging to the Estate upon the plantation is pd away I know not who as yet

2

will give a good acoot for that & a great house kept it is I that according to my promise to the deed must & will from time to time question
those that shall have the Estate for an account
Directed to Mr Toby Smith

Note:
        The foregoing letter, the first entry in Record Book #2 is given in
full. It gives a certain understanding of the character of Edwin Conway
and will be of interest to many of his innumerable Virginia descendants.
The Roman Catholic suggestion here was doubtless on account of his affilia-
tion with Wm. Eltonhead, who lost his life from activities concerning that
faith in Maryland.

p.2 . Appraisal of the estate of Elias Edmonds, late of Corotoman River
in the county of Lancaster, dec'd, the 26th of June 1654. Total value 9211
Tobo.   signed Edwin Connaway
                                   The mark of Wm. Clapham, Sonr.
                                   John Edwards.

p.4. A just and true acoot of Elias Edmonds crop made in the year of our
Lord God 1653 how it is disposed of by the administrator of the sd Edmonds
Estate.

Impr for a maid servt bought for	1600
pd by order of Court to Mr Connaway	300
pd to Mr Forset	340
pd for 2 pr of bodice for the childrens use	50
pd for 4 pr of shoes for the children	56
pd for 1 pr of Stockings of the Boy	14
pd for a petticoat & a pair of breeches for the children	50
pd for 4 yds L- - shirts for the children at 15 p. yd	60
	- - - - -
	2471

John Meredith
Walter (mark) Herd administrators

p.5. Whereas Thos Stephens late of this colony died intestate having an
Estate x x whereof Elizabeth the relict of the sd Stephens has admr granted
by the governor. Signed at James City 17th Nov. 1654 by Richard Bennett,
Governor and Capt. General of Virginia.

p.5. Admr. granted to Lucy Marsh widow of Francis Marsh late of Lancaster
Co. Va., by Gov. Bennett. Signed at James City, 6th April 1653.

p.6. John Greene gives by his will hogs, crop and tobo. to his wife Mary
Greene, and has given his son John Greene 200 acres of land and desires
Andrew Gilson to keep the child.
        Jurat in circa prima Mar 1654 Test John Carter
Witnesses: Andrew Gilson, Jno.Smith.

p.6. "Inventory of goods servants & cattle of Mr George Eaton decd praised by the request of Mr John Hunt admr by us whose names are under- written x x "

A servant by name Thomas Goose having 1 1/2 yr to serve
jo Fookes having 1 1/2 yr to serve
Anthony Web having 2 1/2 yr to serve
Peter Johnson having 4 1/2 yr to sorve
Jo Johnson having 3 1/2 yr to serve
1 servant being run away 6 mos.   Total value   16.601 Tobo.

                    Henry Fleet   David Fox
                    Richd.Furman   Jo Sharpe
                           12 die 8 mo 1653

p.8. Will of Robert Chambers. Refers to "a Barke I bought of James Brown of Charles Town in New England my will is that my Land lord of Boston William Mery shall dispose of as thus that what Mr Garland shall make Just- ly appear to be Due him William Merry to go give satisfaction to my Land- lady Crabtree for a venture of 20 pounds of sugar which I was to be accountable for and for the rest that shall remain of the Barke that shall be in the said William Merry hands I do will it to be distributed to the poor of Gods church in Boston in New England x x x my loving friend Jo Weir to sell my great shallop & to carry home with him of the sale of the sd shallop 2000 lb of tobo the sd tobo to be sold for money & to be equally distributed by the sd Jo Weir to my friends that is to my mother in Law my three aunts and my sister Elizabeth I give to Francis Weir a steer that is at John Rogers at Chickacone I give to Hanner Place for looking to me in my sickness a yearling Heiffer 3 yards of green - - my chest & a -- skin I give unto one honest poor man named Jo Hill living about Kent or Sevurne 1100 lb of tobo due to me by bills from James Dasher of herring creek x x one bill x x to one Richard Paille I give unto Anthony Fullyham (for un- changable love & kindness past betwixt us) one of those Hhds of tobo that I have at his house I give unto Mrs Taylor in consideration of her charge & endeavor to cure me of my Infirmities one cow that is at Mr Fullyhams." Appoints John Weir Exor. Refers to debt to Mr. Scarborough and to debt owing him by Mrs. Crow. Dated 4th February 1653/4.
Wit. Richard Coleman.   signed Robert Chambers.
      Thomas Win . . .   Prob. 10th April 1654.

p.9. Will of Francis Marsh, dated 9th Dec. 1651. To wife Lucy Marsh 200 acres adjoining the upper side of Richd. Loes. Also the balance of estate.
Wit. More Fantleroy   signed Francis (mark) Marsh
     John Edcombe   Prob. 10th April 1653.

p. 10. Will of Robert Mascall. To William Newsom and John Pine a bill of 3000 lb of tobo. To Epaphroditus Lawson a bill of Richard Jones of 2300 lb. tobo. Calf to Mary Tomson. Calf to Robert Nowsom son of William Newsom. Refers to 150 lb tobo due from Charles Snead and 100 lb due from Domenic Theriatt. To Richard Coleman 180 lb tobo due from Jas. Butt. Also 5 shil. to Coleman. To Thos Hanks one sow. To Robert Tomson my best gray suit. Dated 27th Sept 1653. Signed Robert (mark) Mascall.
Wit. Thomas Hank
      Robert Parr   "Jurat octavo Novembris 1653
                          Will Gooch, Comr of Yorke County."

p. 11. Will of Thomas Saxe. Cattle to Dorothy Downman, widow. Cattle to Richard Dudley second son of Edward Dudley. To Mary Tomson dau of Robert Tomson. Furniture etc to Mary Tomson wife of Robert Tomson. To Mr Lampkin and cattle to Lampkin's wife. A sow shoat to Richard Hugh servant to Wm Masham. Exors. Wm. Masham and John Pine. No date.

Wit. Howell Powell   signed   Thomas Sax
      Edward Dudley   Prob 1th January 1654/5.

* p. 12. Will of Thomas Mead. Dated 5th March 1654/5. Wife exor. "my dau. Mary the plantation I now live on at her mothers death." "my two sons Tho: & John Meads" all the land on the W. side of the creek. "My two daughters Margaret & Joyce." To "my daughter Anne" all the cattle now belonging to her "which is about 5 head of cattle & likewise I do give unto her one shilling in money". Balance of property divided among others mentioned.   signed   Thomas Mead.

Wit. Rawleigh Travers
      John Richardson
      Edward (mark) Bradshaw   Prob. 12th June 1655.

p. 12. "I John Meredith shipwright" admtr of est. of Elias Edmonds lately decd, aquits Walter Heard from any part or parcel of the estate of the sd Edmonds.   Rec. 12th June 1655.

Wit. Howell Powell
      William (mark) Thatcher.

p. 13. "The Estate of William Downman is debtor to me Jo Nicholes x x the sume of 922 lb of tobo"   signed   Dority (mark) Downman

Wit Tho. Hacket
    Ric Denham   Rec. " -- die Junij 1655"

p. 14. Re. settlement of the estate of Wm. Downman: "The widow hopes that the Court will be so pleased to bestow her bed & that belongeth to upon her having not anything to lie upon & she shall ever pray for their worships felicity."   signed   Thomas Hacket
                             Edwin Conniway
         Rec.   12 die Junij 1655.

p. 14. Wm. Underwood sells cattle to Edward Bradshaw.

Wit. Wm. Mosley
      George Baules   Rec. 6th June 1655.

p. 14. Power of Atty, Edward (mark) Bradshaw to Mr. Hum. Booth to sue Wm. Cotton. Dated 29th March 1655.

Wit. William Underwood
      William Ball   Rec. 6th June 1655.

p. 15. Mortgage. Abraham Moone of Lanc. Co. to Thos. Hanks. Plantation, servants etc. bought of Edward Diggs, Esqr. Dated 10 Feb 1654/5. Refers to Moone's wife, does not give her name.
Wit. John Buckner
  Erasmus Chamley   Rec. "6 die Junij 1655"
"Post Script
  Mr Phillips pray ack the aforesaid deed for my use to the bearer as my real act & deed   Yors Abra Moone "

p. 15. An Inventory of debts remaining unpaid of Mr Epa Lawsons Estate June the 5th 1655.
  Hen Knowles
  John Edgecombe to Walters
  Mr Jo Englishs a/c
  Jo Gatlin to Ed Walter 500 10d nails.
  Ed Walter
  Capt Franc Giles bond
  Ed Asheroff
  Jo Giles
  Ric Meade
  Mr Toby Smith
  Franc Marsh
  John Smith 5 bbl corn
  Jo Dodman
  Portor Toler (Peter Taler ?)
  Philip Bayley
  Anto Davy (Anto Dony ?)
  Jo Smith
  Jo Edcombe
  Jo Cable
  Anti Dony to Epa Bonnison
  Fran Barnes
  Michael Bridges
  An Burt
  Will Harper
  Hen Read
  Ed Hughes for Mr Rinsy
  Will - -dding   Total   15804

  Pd to Mr Lawson as in the accot to Mr Toby Smith debt 1500

and 500 10d nailes of Mr John Carter   Rec "12 Junij 1655"

p. 15 Inventory of Est. of Paul Brewer late decd. of Lanc. Co.
      Total val. 7267 tobo.
signed Ro Younge, John (mark) Beeby, George (mark) Kilman.
Jas. Bagnell
"A note what debts pd by me Wm Johnson for Paul Brewer this present year unto

Mr Ja Williamson	864	Oliver Seger	700
Mr Jollson	547	John Kapell	300
Mr Jackman	700	bill to myself	160
Mr Grufin(Griffin)	700		

     Rec. "10 die 9ber 1655"

p. 18. Will of John Phillips. Whole estate to wife Sarah. Friend Moore
Fantleroy (Fauntleroy) to be Admr. Dated 30th Oct.1655.
Wit. Vincent Stanford   signed   Jo Phillips
      James Yates his marke   Rec. "10 die February 1655" (1655/6)

p. 18.   3rd Feb. 1654/5. Abraham Moone to Walter Bartlet for one cow calf.
Assigned to James Mackrum 3rd March 1655/6.

p.18.   Power of Atty Ed Streator to John Sharpe to receive from Maj.
Carter the - - - of Capt. Brocas bill. Dated 21 Jan. 1655/6.
Wit. Jo. Washington   Rec "3 Marij 1655" (1655/6)

p. 19.   "Major John Carter Sr These may certify to you I gave power to Mr
Thomas Bushrode to receive a certain debt from your - - - or Capt Brocas
unto Mr Fairwaites & company these are to desire you to make payment unto
this bearer Mr John Ashley as you and he can agree & this note shall be your
sufficient warrent and his acquittance your full discharge from the sd debt
                    by your Lo: friend George Jordan
Ja the 31st 1655" (1655/6)

p. 19.   Deed John Meredith, shipwright of Lanc. Co. to Walter Dikeson.
600 acres on "Eastward side of the Eastward branch of Corotomen River
bought of Majr John Bond" . Dated 1st Feb. 1655/6.
                              signed Jo Merrideth his seale
Wit. Howell Powell
      Tho Powell   Rec. by Jo Sharpe attor. of Meredith,
                          "3 Marij 1655" (1655/6)

p.20.   Deed Thos Ball of the County of Northampton in Virginia, marriner,
to John Jones of the same place, planter. One patent 350 a. land lying in
Corotoman River in Rappahannock bought of John Edwards, Chirurgeon, about
two years past. Dated 15th No. 1655.
Wit. Anto Hodgkins   signed   Tho Ball & seale
      Edwd Rendel   Ack. 6 Feb.1655/6
                           Rec   3 Mar 1655/6

p. 21.   Deed . Enock Hawker of Lanc. Co. to Nicholas Haile of same Co,
planter, 500 a. being 1/2 of 1000 a. patented by sd. Hawkins (sic) and
Anthony Davy.   Dated 6th Feb. 1655/6.
Wit. Willm White   Ack   6th Feb. 1655/6
      Tho Hardinge   Rec   3rd Mar. 1655/6.

p.21. Deed. John Meredith to Mr John Jones 300 acres. Dated 9 Apl.1656.
Wit. Edmund Lunn
        Vinc Stanford   Ack. 15 Apl. 1656   Rec. 12 June 1656.

p. 22. Power of Atty. Simon Overzee of Linhaven,merchant, to William
Underwood to collect debts in Rappahannock. Dated 16 Feb. 1655/6
Wit. Rowland Lawson
        Tho Harvey his mark.   Rec. 12 June 1656.

p.22.   Will of Arthur Dunn. My godson Chichester Hobert the son of
Bartram Hobert 300 a. of land purchased from Abraham Moone. To Richard
and Mary the two children of John Welch a cow calf to each. To friend
Thomas Kidd two cows. To friend Bartram Hobert cattle, bed sheets "and
what else I bought of Robt. Middleton. To Anthony Barlow one old white
sow. Debt to be paid in cash to Wm. Ball. Various other items, crops,
cattle etc. to Thos. Kidd and Bartram Hobert. To Mrs. Wyllis stock "about
Mr Wyllis house". Refers to debt due him from Mr. Myles Dixon. To Mr.
Obert (sic) my black bull. Loving friends Bartram Hobert and Thos Kidd
exors. Dated 16 Nov. 1655.
Wit. Willm Ball   signed Arthur Dunn (seale)
        Tho Widd his marke   Rec. 12 April 1656.

p. 24. Deed. Richd Parrott and Margaret Parrott to Minor Minson and Robt
Kempe 300 a. on S. side of Rappahannock. Dated 12 Jan. 1655/6.
Wit. John Vause
        Dan Welsh his mark   Ack 6th Mar 1655/6 Rec. 12 Apl.1656

p.25. Release of Walter Herd by Thomas Powell and Howell Powell 400 acres.
Wit Walter Dickinson
        John Merredith   Ack. 15 Apl.1656   Rec 12 June 1656.

p.25. John Carter of Rappahannock gives "my two children John and
Elizabeth my ten negroes named x x x"
Wit. Wm. Underwood
        Tho Bristoe   Ack. 15 Apl.1656   Rec. 12 June 1656.

p.26.   John Vause to Richard Blewford 300 acres according to patent the
said John Vause and Willm Veale bought of Richard Coleman.
Dated 21 Nov.1655.   signed   Jo Vause (the seale)
Wit. Thomas Evans
        Willm Rice   Ack. 15 Apl. 1656 Rec. 12 June 1656.

8

p.26. John Gillet to Jos Bayly 200 a. on Rappahannock "of which divident
one Mr Best hath 500 x x x and Jo Smithy 200" acres. Dated 4th Feb. 1655/6.
Wit. Rich Harrowd   signed Jo Billett the seale (sic)
     Ed Parkely   Jane Billett (sic)
                        Rec 12 June 1656.
(Note: We would assume this name to be Gillett, possibly recorded in error)

p.27. Walter Dickeson to John Irish 500 acres on W. of Corotoman River.
Dated 17 Jan 1654/5   signed Walter Dickeson the seale
Wit. Jo Phillips
     Jo Edwards   Ack 15 Apl 1656   Rec. 12 June 1656.

p.28 Appraisal of estate of Abraham Moone 23rd Feb. 1655/6.
                    Total value   15.222 tobo.
A list of debts due the estate:
Rowland Hibben & Dorothy Butler their bill for   2500
Bill of Tho Hardinge   800
Jo Irish his bill for a man servant
Tho Griffin his bill for 4 shoats
Robt Younge his bill
Isaac Richardson
Tho Ballard his bill for 30 yds of buckram
Arthur Dunn
Jo Phillips
Capt Fleet his bill for 10 barrels of corne
Capt Fleets bill for 9 barrels more
Mr Toby Smithes bill for the rights of 1600 a of land & 110 lb of tobo
Walter Dickesons bill
Jo Nicholls
James Butts
Humphrey Haggetts bill
Enock Hawkers bill
Mr Geo Colcloughs bill
Jo Edwards bill
Tho Hopkins bill
Jo Merediths bill
Capt Haggotts bill
Tho Powells bill
Geo Waddings bill
Mr Grymes his note to be accountable for bills of 589 more upon the note
        for the survey of Gwins Iland 600 a bill of sale for 2 heifers with
        their increase from Tho Burne   1200
Capt Pensax his bill for 2 steers he recd
                        Total 18152 tobo.
Appraisal Dated 23rd Feb 1655/6
                        signed   Tho Carter
                                 Willm Leech
                                 Cuthbert Potter
                                 Dennys Conyer
More a note of Coll Makums for the delivery of a horse and 13 head of
        cattle
                Exhib 15 April 1656 Rec. 20 April 1656.

p. 31.   Bartholomew Hoskins of Elizabeth River, planter, in the county
of Lower Norfolk to John Greene of London, merchant, 600 acres on the S.
side of Rappahannock, part of 1350 acres patented by the sd Hoskins. The
patent issued by " Sr Wm Berkley Kt & Governor then of this colony of
Virginia". Dated 13th Oct. 1655.
Wit. jo Smith   signed Barth Hoskins the seale
       Richard Richardson
"Countryman Thrush
       I shall intreat you to acknowledge this bill of sale which I have made
to Mr Greene for his Land at Rappahannock in Court in my behalfe and this
my note shall be your sufficient warrant therein and that it be according
to your mind so Just   Your lo Friend
From Eliz River this   Barth Hoskins
21st of Decembr 1655"
                          Ack 15th April 1656   Rec 12 June 1656.

p.32. "Item I give unto my cousin Nicholas White 150 acres of land adj
to the land of William Johnson x x " Dated 23 Feb. 1655/6.
Wit.   Edward Britton   signed   Jo: Cox
       Fran Overton His mark
"likewise I give Edward Bretton power in my absence to see it recorded"
                          Ack 6 March 1655/6   Rec 16 June 1666

p.33   Will of Edward Bradshaw. To Capt. Moore Fanteleroy cattle. To John
Jones son of Rice Jones cattle, To Winnefred Griffin daughter of Thomas
Giffen (Griffen) one cow. To Jone daughter in law to Rice Jones a chest,
"wastecoat", etc. To Thomas Griffin "my countryman" 8 hhd tobo. I sold to
Mr Travers the next years pay and likewise my servant etc. Also "all
other goods that is betwixt me & Mr Underwood. Thos Griffin Exor. To
Vincent Stanford 300 lb tobo. Dated Jan.17th 1655/6.
Wit. Reynold Johnson   signed Edward Bradshaw
      Arthur Clarke his mark   his mark
      Anne Garritt her mark
      Vincent Stanford   Rec 17 Jun. 1656. Edwd. Dale, clerk.

p. 34.   Grant to John Robinson. 250 acres in Co. of Lanc on S. side of
Rappahannock adjoining land of John Sharpe on S.E., on N.W. by the cliffs
on N.E by Rapp. River, on S.W. by the woods. For transportation of five
persons, names not shown, into the colony. Dated 29 Nov.1652.
                          signed Rich Bennett
                                  W Clayborne Sec.

p.35. Jno. Robinson sells to Charles Hill, for valuable consideration
recd in hand "by one Jno Robbinson of John Mullings " the foregoing 150
(sic) acres of land. Dated 7 Oct.1653.
Wit Philip Stevenson   signed   Jo Robinson his marke
     Hum Booth   Ack. 6 Aug.1656 Rec 8 Aug.1656

p.35. Richd Lawson of the County of Lancaster, gent. to Wm Hall of the
County aforesaid, cooper, 1400 acres "I now liveth upon" on So. side of
Lawson's Creek. Dated June 30 1656.
Wit. Toby Smith   signed   Richd Lawson   his seale
     The mark of Peter Taylor
" I Elizabeth Lawson the wife of Richd Lawson de acknowledge the sale of
the Land above mentioned & do hereunto set my hand 3rd September 1656
                                        Elizabeth Lawson"
                    Recog. 3 Sept. 1656 Rec. 23 Sept. 1656.

p.36.   Grant,14th June 1655, by Edward Digges, Esq., to Franc Gower (sic)
530 acres situated in Co. of Lanc. on S. side of Rappa. River on the East-
ward side of Hodskins Creek. 250 acres of this formerly granted Mr. Ja
Williamson who assigned it to Goare (sic). Refers further to Francis
Goare. 280 acres of this patent ack. in Court by Francis Gower unto
Thomas Pettit.   signed   Edward Digges
                                              W Claiborne Secr
                         Rec. 23 September 1656.

p.36.   James Williamson of Rappahannock, merchant, to Ambrose Meather of
Rappahannock, 1000 acres. Dated 3rd Sept. 1656.
Wit. Ja Bagnal   signed Ja Williamson his seale
     Will Johnson
     Edward Dale   Rec. 28th October 1656.
Ambrose Meather ack. in Court 600 acres of above to Tho Robbinson.
                         Rec. 28th October 1656.

p.38.   Will of William Carne. Dated 18th July 1656. To John Waterman
and Willm Frisle debt due from Thomas Berfoot. Refers to debts due him
from Francis Gaines, Dunkyn Roy, Geo Affeld, John C- -, Patrick Miller,
James Bonner, John Bell, Richard Harper. Desires that debts be paid, due
by him to Leut Coll Ellis (?), Andrew Cerliff and to Coll Guinn.
Wit. John Bell   signed   the mark of Willm Carne
      the mark of Jo Needles
"Postcript In case the sd Willm Frizell be alive it doth belong half to
him if not it doth belong all to Jo Waterman."
                         Recorded 23rd September 1656.

p.39.   Inventory of George Beach, decd. Total 2589 lb. tobc. Dated 24th
June 1656.   signed   Peter Montague
                                          Willm Needham
                                          Hump Booth
                    Recorded 23rd September 1656.

p.40. An addition to the Inventory of Capt. B- - - estate to be
appraised by order of Court by Mr William Tignor, Mr Wm Leech and Mr
Hobart. Total val. 10100 lb. tobo.

             signed Will Tignors mark
                      Will Leechs mark
                      Barhan Hobart
          Recorded 23 Sept 1656.

p.40. Power of Atty from Robt Snead to Capt Moore Fanteleroy to collect
sum of tobo "due me out of estate of Abraham Moone for x x expenses in his
sickness & for his funeral." Dated March 19 1655/6.
Wit. Vino Stanford   Recorded 23rd Sept.1656.

p. 40. Will of Walter Flemminge. Dated 24th Nov.1655. Refers to cattle
left at Mr Rowland Lawsons and an agreement with Mr Robert Burrill. To
Robert Burrill cattle. To my loving friend Hugh Brent tobo due from Will
Wilkinson at Coretoman. Refers to tobo due from John Brathall, from
Mr Geo. Marshe and from Mr Thomas Medstone. "Mr Lawsons the yearlings at
his pen the chest in his house and my cloathes I give to Mr Burrill
his son for diverse favors which he hath done for me". Further bequest
"to my loving friend Hugh Brent."
Wit.   signed Tho marke of
The marke of Isaac Walker   Walter Flemminge
The marke of Elleanor Walker
          Recorded 23rd Sept.1656.

p.41. Deposition of Isaac Weaver (sic) (Walker ?) aged 47 years or there-
abouts of Northumberland County, taken before Mr Nicholas Morrys & Richd.
Budd, both Commissioners, re estate of Fleming.
Wit. Nicholas Morris
    R Budd
Deposition of Elleanor Walker, aged 34 or thereabouts, of Northumborland
County, regarding Walter Fleming desiring to give 4 bbl. corn to Mr
Rowland Lawson after he had signed his will.
Wit. Nicholas Morrys
    James Hawley   Exhib. 6 Feb.1655/6. Rec. 23 Sept.1656.

p.42. Inventory of estate of Jo Philips, decd., appr. by Mr. Rawleigh
Travers & Mr Tho Griffith (sic) the 30th of Jan. 1655/6.
Total val. 4535 lb. tobo.   signed Rawleigh Travers
                          Tho Griffin his marke (sic)
          Exhib. 6 Mar 1655/6 Rec.23rd Sept. 1656.

p.42. "John Bell before his death did by word of mouth give unto the
Widd Bryant & her children 2 yearling calves and to his countryman afterwards naming Alexander Porteus at Morattico his boat for a rememborance
and to Thomas who was his mate liberty to plant upon his land this
year and the rest of his Estate he gave to Cipryan B P (shown thus, the
person referred to was Ciprtian Bishop) signed James Bagnell
                       John Gregory
"Jurat in Cur 14 Jan 1656 recordat 20 Jan 1656" (1656/7)

p. 43 This entry faded and difficult to read. Inventory of Nicholas Forman (?) decd. Total 5209 tobo.   signed Rawleigh Travers
Tho Griffin
"Exhib in Ct by Hum Booth 14 ja 1656"

p. 44. Mr Williamsons a/c of Toby Hursts estate.
Items include:
to Rich Tomlinson   30
By a sheet to bury him   40
for a pound of thread   24
for a gallon of brandy
for a gallon of alligant   30

Total 4410 tobo
Exhib 14 Jan 1656 Rec 20 Jan 1656
Edward Dale, Clerk.

p. 45.   Will of Dennys Conyers. To Lambert Moore land, he to remain and care for stock etc. To Mr Myles Dixon & Mr Cuthbert Potter " a case of sack & a fat barrow to be made use of according to a promise between them and me". To "my loving friend Mr Cuthbert Potter" 100 acres of land formerly sold to Peter Godson. "To my cousin Dennys Conyers now servant to Coll Matthews" land. "He failing in heirs to Leiu Coll Tho Ludlowe and Mr Cuthbert Potter whom I make overseers of my Estate x x x until such time as a lawful heir to me does come to make a claimthereof." To Lt. Coll. Thos. Ludlowe a ring of 20 shillings, the same to Mrs. Mary Potter. "my loving friends" Ludlowe and Potter to be overseers.
Dated 3rd Oct.1656.   signed Dennys Connyers his marke.
Wit.   Tho Chetwood
Jno Walker   Proved 4th Feb 1656/7.

Note: If a man of the family standing and wit of Dennis Conyers was unable to write his name, then, Robert Beverley notwithstanding and the school teachers to the contrary, being able to read and write was certainly not the necessary accomplishment of a gentleman of this period in Virginia or in England. The Conyers arms were quartered to such an extent with old English families that their delineation was nothing short of a nuisance. Beverley Fleet.

Note #2. The taking of these abstracts has not been altogether for the enlightenment of genealogists as dull and self centered as myself. There is there must be- in these old records the key to the Virginia character. Among other things a fist backed by a stout arm has its place. Now in 1656 DEATH was an awesome spectre. Our Mr. Conyers seems to have been amused and to have the courage to laugh and have his friends make merry in his very face. So did others, including General Morgan years later. Perhaps a laugh will undo years of priggish study. Let us be careful and beware. Beverley Fleet.

p.46. Will of Rowland Burnham of Rappahannock in Virginia intending
to make a voyage to England in the ship Anthony of London.

To my brother Thomas Holmes of York River and to my sister
Margery Holmes his wife, each 20 shillings to buy a ring.

To my loving friend Francis Cole of Rappahannock River and to
Alice Cole his wife, 20 shillings each to buy a ring and to her (Alice
Cole) ten pounds to be laid out in plate for her own use.

To my son John Burnham a negro boy and to my daughter Elleanor
Burnham a negro girl.

Unto my two eldest sons Thomas and John Burnham, two English
youths called Timothy Doner and Edmond, both of them for the full term
of tyme they have to serve. Also negro slaves.

To my daughter Eleanor Burnham and to my son Fran. Burnham
three English servants called John Henley, David Watkins and John Lewys,
also negro slaves.

To my sons John Burnham, Francys Burnham and to my daughter
Elleanor Burnham one half of all my stock, etc. As for my son Thomas
Burnham he hath sufficient stock of cattle of his own.

To my sons Thomas, John and Francys Burnham and to my daughter
Eleanor Burnham 1/2 of my hogs, 2/3 of crop. The other 1/3 to belong
to their mother, Alice Burnham my wife.

Tobo. "to be shipped under my old mark unto Mr Jefferys & Mr
Colclough in London."

Land on S. side of Rappahannock where I now live "When my son
Thomas shall come to the age of 20 years he the said Thomas shall at
the division have his first choice in regard of his birthright."

To wife Alice a number of bequests including "all the plate I
have in the house." also "seventy pounds sterling which is in her
custody" and "all such plate as shall come out of England for her this
year."

Further bequests to "my four above named children."

Other bequests to his wife "during her widowhood & no longer
but then to depart without injuring the houses or drawing a naile about
or in any of them."

"my loving friend Francis Cole and my brother Thomas Holmes exors."
Dated 12th February 1655/6.
Wit. Francis Cole his mark   signed   Row Burnham.
     John Vause
     Robert Taylor   Rec. 1st March 1656/7. Edwd Dale clerk.

Note: Alice Eltonhead, one of the sisters who made such remarkably good
matches in early Virginia, married 1st Rowland Burnham and, very shortly
after his death, 2nd the wealthy Henry Corbin. We sincerely hope this
worldly ancestress of ours did not fill one of her silver bowls with nails
in departing. She married 3rd, Captain Henry Creek (Creyk) of a good old
Yorkshire family. B.F.

p.49. Account of debts paid by Elleanor Beach, widow of George Beach,
her husband, decd. to Mr Fox 1200, to Robert Gray 400. Total 1600 tobo.

Account of the goods of her children which were sold by George Beach,
her husband, decd., woh the Court hath ordered she should be satisfied in
the first place. The list includes: to Jo Robinson
                                        to Mr Booth
                                        childrens toys   100
                                        Total   4780 tobo.
                               signed Elleanor Beach her mark.
                               Recorded 1st March 1656/7.

14

p.50. Inventory of Est. of John Johnson Senr. Total 2518 tobo.
signed Barham Hobert
Tho Wyllys
Sworn in Court 7th Dec.1655.

Along with the above, on page 51, is an inventory of the Est. of
John Johnson the younger, late decd., taken Dec. 17th 1656. Includes 300
lb. of tobo. due from Wm Copeland.
signed Vinc Stanford
Rich Lewys
Both exhib. in Court by Thomas Wyllys 4th Feb. 1656/7
Recorded 1st March 1656/7.

p.51. Alice Burnham, widow and relict of Mr. Rowland Burnham appointed
admx of his est. by Edward Digges, Esq., Governor and Capt. General of
Virginia. Dated James Citty 1st March 1656/7. Recorded 7th April 1657.

p.52. The a/c of Abraham Moone estate given in by John Curtys who made
these several payments following:

To Mr Meriwether	6784
Mr Hubbard	5600
Mr Fox	2180
James Mackmun	200
Will Copeland	1318
Edward Simpson a/c man serv	2000
Mr Brereton a/c fees	1303
Vincent Stanford	956
Mr Bries	400
Grace Sanderson	1200
Vinc Stanford	470
Illegible - -	1110
funeral charge	2000
Court Levys	275
Mr - - ernen	6000
Mr Booth	3600
Edward Digges Esq	1800
Mr Boncley (?)	1950
Mr Dale for fees	1719
james Allison a/c corne & cloaths	1000
Total	41885 tobo.

Recorded 10th Feb. 1656/7

p.53. Will of Thomas Bries of Rappahannock in Va. To wife, Martha Bries,
all estate in England and in Virginia. She sole exor. Dated 24 Apl.1657.
Wit. Davy Fox
Thomas Hasler
Edward Dale   Proved 19th May 1657.

p.54. Debts paid by Tobias Horton out of the est. of John Taylor, decd.

for use of Coll Willm Clayborne	2500
for use of Mr Bennett	740
for Wm Hancocks use	610
to Abraham Moone	1150
to Mr Marsh and Court charges	673
more for charges arrested to James Towne	500
Total	6173

Exhibit in Curt 29 July 1657 by Tobias Horton   Red. 1 Aug.1657.

p.54.   Will of Francys Cole of the Co. of Lanc. in Rappa. River. To
wife Alice Cole plantation during widowhood. To my two daughters Francys
and Mary Cole. To Francis Browne the son of Francis Browne a calf. To my
servant John Burroughs. To Mr Roger Radford one suit of clothes and one
heifer with calf. Exors wife and dau. Frances. Dated 1st July 1658.
Wit. Roger Radford   signed Fran: Cole
     Edward Dale.   Prob. 29th Sept 1658.

p.56.   " Hannah Hood aged 24 years or thereabouts sworn and examined
saigth that Roger Radford decd did in the time of his sickness say I give
my Land to Doll (meaning Mary Cole the Daughter of the Widd Cole) & none
other shall have it & further sayeth not
29th Sept. 1658   signed   Hannah Hood."

p.56.   "Will Price can swear to the best of his knowledge (vizt) I came
into the room where Mr Radford was seting upon his sick bed I asked him
how he did pretty well he said you are not I think - -illegible- - for
this world therefore you had best make your peace with God & to set
everything to rights with Mr Cooke he answered no for he is more ingaged
to me than I to him what do you give Doll Cole your Land I I (sic) give
Doll Cole my Land God forbid but that she should have that how often
shall I tel you I give Doll Cole my Land
                        signed   Will Price."
                 Recorded 1st October 1658.

p.57.   " Jo Edwards cooper aged 30 or thereabouts sworn sayeth That
Will Blunherd upon his death bed did give unto his landlady one hhd of
tobo & to her child one yearling calf & three shoats more". to John Potter
clothing and to Mr Ellyott timber and "for the rest of his Estate he gave
to his mates"   signed John Edwards
                 Dated 29th Sept 1658.   Rec. 1st Oct.1658.

p.57.   "Abigall Duckett aged 21 yere or thereabouts sworn sayeth That
Will Blunherd upon his death bed did call her master and sayed Mr Vincent
you have all in your own hands pay yourself to the full and afterwards he
gave to his landlady one hhd of tobo & to her child x x x".
                 signed   Abigall Duckett
                 Dated 29th Sept 1658.   Rec 1st Oct.1658

p.57.   Will of Vincent Sranford of the Co. of Lanc. in Va. "I give
& bequeath towards the purchaseing of a glebe for the par'sh wherein
I now live one thousand pounds of good tobo and caske to be paid within
two years of my decease." To the widd Dudley 1 hhd tobo. To my neice
Lydia the wife of Anthony Tibboe cattle. To Mary the dau of Mr Edward
Dale 800 acres lying on Lawsons Creek. To Mary my wife balance of estate.
Exors Mr Edward Dale "& Mary my aforesd wife." Dated 16 Nov.1658.
                              signed   Vincent Stanford.
Wit. Robert Pollard
     Elyas Wilson
28th Nov.1658 Edward Dale, Maria Stanford wid and Robert Pollard.
                    Recorded 1st October 1658 (sic)
Probate granted by the right honbl Will Berkeley Knt unto Mary the wid
and relict of the above named Vin Stanford Dated at James City the 20th
of March 1659.

p.59. Will of Henry Rye. To my son Will Rogers bed etc. "and this my son
to Tho Philips to use him as his own." "a bill in my chest of five hundred weight of tobo to satisfy Willm Harper the next October fifty nine."
To Mr Peter Knight 300 wt of tobo. Dated 20th Feb.1658/9.
Wit Tho Bunbury   signed Hen Rye
     Ed Lunsford   Prob. by testam of Thos Phillips & Edwd Lunsford
                              30th March 1659.

p.59.   Will of Randolph Chamblett. Dated 15th Jan. 1658/9. To the child
of Mary Bennett 4 cows. To my godson Randolph Seager a calf. To Daniel
Johnson a cow. To Geo. Marsh 30 shillings for a ring. To Anne Thatchwell
"plantation I now live upon about 100 acres of Land" with houses etc.
Debts to be paid and balance of estate to Anne Thatchwell, she to be exor.
No witnesses   signed   Randolph Chamblett
Prob "granted Thatchwell widd" March 20th 1659. (1658/9 ?)

p.60.   Will of Olliver Segar. To my eldest son Olliver Segar, my houses
and Lands, they to remain in the hands of my wife Elleanor Segar until
he comes to age. Balance of estate to be divided betw wife and three
children, Olliver, Elizabeth and Randolph. Exors beloved friends Mr,
Richard Lee and Nicholas Cooke. Dated 24th Jan.1658/9.
Wit. Anne Thatchwell   signed   Olliver Segar.
     Jane Curtys
     Nicho Cooke   Prob 30 March 1659

p.61.   Will of "Margaret Grymes of the County of Lancaster widow in
Virginia." To Willm Baughton my son, cattle. To Tho Baughton son of
Will Baughton, cattle and slave. To my daughter Anne White, bed cloth-
ing, dishes etc. To "my son Will White my son in Law" one boy servant.
To "my son Wraughton" (sic) furniture. Dated 18th Feb.1658/9.
Wit   Rich George   signed   Margarett Grymes.
      Tho Marshall
           Prob by "Willi Wroughton" Richi George and Tho Marshall,
                              30th March 1659.

p.62. Will of Peter Montague. Dated 27th March 1659. To my wife Cicely 1/3 of estate. To my two sons Peter and Will Montague all my lands lying in Rappahannock River, they failing in heirs to my three daughters Ellen, Margaret and Elizabeth and the child of Anne late wife of John Jadwyn. To my four children Peter, Will, Margaret and Elizabeth 2/3 of personal estate. To my daughter Ellen the wife of Will Thompson, 1000 lb of tobo out of 1300 lb he owes me. Exors wife Cicely and son Peter.
Wit   George Marsh
       Thomas James   Prob. 1st July 1659.

p.63.   Inventory of estate of Mr John Irish, decd. taken 10th Apl.1659.
Total 3321 tobo.   signed   Will Ball
                                  John Sharpe
                                  Tho Powell
                Recorded 1st July 1659

p.64. "James Bonner aged about 30 years or thereabouts sworn and examined sayeth about the last of April being with Mr Thomas Prettyman two or three days before his death he said Mr Matthew Kempe to have all he had."
Sworn before us   signed   James Bonner.
Henry Fleete
Rowland Lawson   Recorded 27th July 1659.

p.64.   Bridget Bonner aged about 24 years sworn and examined re Thomas Prettyman as above.
Sworn before us
Henry Fleete
Rowland Lawson   Recorded 27th July 1659.

p.65.   Will of Will Angell. To my son Uria Angell and to my two daus Margaret Angell and Alice Angell. The two daus under age. That Alexander Nash be paid hhd of tobo I owe him. That L- - Johnson be paid 2 Ells of canvas I owe him. Dated 20th Oct.1659.
Wit. Hugh Brent   signed   Will Angell
      Abya Bonnison
Prob by Hugh Brent, Ebby Bonnison and Uria Angell 30th November 1659.

p.65.   Will of Thomas Duncombe of Lanc. Co. To wife Mary Duncombe. She exor. Dated 9th Sept 1659.
Wit   Robert Smith
      Samuell Heron   Prob. 30th November 1659.

p.66.   Will of Abraham Appleton. Refers to small tools at Mrs Oberts and at Rich Lewys. Tobo at Will Neeshams. "x x at all demands five and twenty shills for the coffin with Mr Corbyn." Tobo at Tho Williams and at John Welsh. Refers to work Ive done at Mrs Obert. Apparently does not give any-one anything excepting to Rich Lewys "2 shirts a pr of drawers a band and a handkerf at Mrs Obert to fetch." Dated 20th Oct 1659.
Wit Will Pow   signed   Abraham Appleton
     Jo Hudds (sic)
Prob by Will Pew and Jo Budds (sic) 30th November 1659.

p.67.   Inventory of Est. of Hannah Mountney, wid. taken 30th Nov.1659.
Not signed.   Recorded 30th November 1659.

p.67. Inventory of Teague Floyne taken 19th Nov. 1659.
                    signed Eliz Sullivan.   Rec.30 Nov.1659.

p.68. Appraisal of Est. of Andrew Butcher. Total 1535 tobo. Dat.15 Oct.
1659   signed   The Wyllys
                            Richd Robinson his marke
                      Recorded 30 Nov. 1659.

p.68.   Inventory of Mr Francis Cole divided according to Order Of Court:
                Belonging to Mary Cole   x x x
                    "   " Mrs Cole   x x x
                    "   " Francis Cole   x x x

Estate of Francis Cole:
                Recd of Mr Montague   380
                  "   " Will Price   300
                  "   " Anne Thatchwell   300
Debts not recd.   Will Denbigh
                    Capt Wilsons note
                        signed George Marsh
                      Recorded 30th Nov. 1659

p.72.   Appraisal of est. of Mr Jo Bayne, decd. Total 2230 tobo.
                        signed   Tho Wyllys
                            Richd Lewys
                  Ex. Rich Robinson 30th Nov. 1659.

p.72.   Will of Barham Obert (Bertram Hobert). To my eldest son Barham
Obert land adj. Richd Lewys, cattle, etc., failing in heirs to son
Chichester. To my dau Lettice Obert. To my next dau Agatha Obert. "the
child my wife now goeth with." My wife Anne Obert during her life all
the rest of my land in Rappa. River. Dated "last day of November 1659."
Wit   Tho Roots   signed Bartram Obert.
    Tho Wyllys   Prob. 25th Jan 1659/60

p. 74.   Inventory of Est. of Willm Angell, decd., taken by Hugh Brent
and Abya Bonnison. 14th Jan 1659/60.
                      Recorded 25th Jan. 1659/60.

p.74.   Will of John Wakefield. To Rowland Haddaway and to Peter
Haddaway, cattle. Dated 25th Aug. 1659.
Wit. John Humphreys   signed   Jno Wakefield his mark
      Edward Bromfield   Recorded 1st May 1660.

p. 75.   Will of Wm. Clapham, Junr. of Rappahannock River in the County
of Lancaster.   To my son William 200 acres "I have contracted for with
Tobyas Horten upon the Land in Haddaways Creek in Fleets Bay". Balance of
estate to be devided betw. "my wife Elizabeth and my son William and Anne
my daughter and my other little infant that my sd wife now goeth with."
Refers to 1500 lb tobo due from Thomas Hunt. Exors wife Elizabeth Clapham
and my brother in Law Thomas Madestard. Dated 16 January 1659/60.
Wit. Thomas Madestaed   signed   Willm Clapham (sic)
      Will Lippert
      T Hunter   Prov. 16th June 1660.

p.76. Prob of will of Olliver Segar, decd, granted to Elleanor his wife
by the right honble Sir Will Berkeley, Kt., Dated at James City 20th Mar.
1659.

p. 76. Commission of Admr granted upon estate of Will Thatchwell, decd.,
March 20th 1659/60.

p.76. Appraisal of est. of Tho Meade late decd July 14th 1655.
Total val. 17502 tobo.   signed   Ambrose Meather
                                            Toby Hurst
                                            Francis Goure
                                            Tho Robinson
                           Rec " 10 die 9bris 1655.

Note: The explanation of the change in the consecutive order of dates
may be found on page 461. Beverley Fleet.

p.77. Debts due to Tho Elgar in Virginia from sundry persons upon
several bills
      " Mr Tully for a practice of piety   20
        John Robins 3 empty hhd   23
        Robert Lovedeath 20 Edward Myell Jane 18 servants
           to Mr Wilkinson of Mycoton (note: this entry seems
           confused but it is shown as well as I was able to
           decipher it. B.F.)   58
        Christo Young   28
        Hen Poole a/c bill   163
        Capt Leo Yeo a/c bill   90
        John Ware a/c 2 bills with cask   393
        Ralph Mourton a/c 2 bills 410 besides 30 & 1 cask 440
(this entry continued on next page)

p. 77 (continued)

Fra Lands a/c bill	130
John Jones a/c bill	80
Tho Goodman Tho Halliard a/c bill with cask	250
Total	1875 "

"Memo That I Tho Cely of London merchant now bound for Virginia have received of the above named Tho Elgar the several bills of the particular debts above specified together with a letter of atturney from him & Joane Dennis his mother to recover & receive the above debts x x" 13th day of August 1639 (note; prob meant for 1659 B.F.)
Wit. Edw Robin   signed   Thomas Cely the scale
     Christo Joyner

p.79.   Power of Atty to Hum Booth of London, merchant, from Fra Fabian of London, merchant, to collect from Robert Bird of Virginia in parts beyond the seas planter x x. Dated "25 day of 7ber 1653."
Wit. Richard Ayres and   signed   Francis Fabian
     Thomas Hinderson   Recorded July 10th 1654.

October 17 1652
    Received of Fra Fabian one bill of Mr John Hammonds of 238 lb of tobo and to receive of "mr Wm'son" 20 lb of tobo; of Mr Ayres 1394 lb of tobo. "Received one black suit and Cloake which is for David Mundaye if he shall deliver to me 900 wt of good tobo & caske x x ."
Wit Samuel Harsell   signed   the mark of
                                                  Robt RB Bird
                            Recorded 10th July 1654.

p. 80.   Mathew Humphreys records a heifer calf for Wm the son of Wm Nichols .   "Recognit in our 6 die 8bris
                        Record 15 die - - - 1654 "

p. 80. The mark of Dennis Coniers cropt & slit on both ears given in and ordered to be recorded.   Rec. "10 Junij 1654"

p.80.   Power of Atty. from John Harawell of London, mercht to Hump Booth of Lond. also mercht to collect debts in Virginia.
Wit.   Rich Chandler
        Tho Booth
        Tho Hindeson   Recorded 10th July 1654.

p.82. Grant by Rich Bennett, Esq., etc., 600 acres on Rappa. adjoining land of Howell Powell, to Rich Colman.   No date shown.
                        signed   Ri Bennett
                                  Wm Clayborne
The above grant made over to Jno Catlet by Rich Colman 30th Mar.1654.
Wit Tho Lucas Junr   signed   Rich Colman.
     Exper Dixon his mark.

p.82. Foregoing grant (p.20) assigned by John Catlet to Tho Page & Nioh
Handley, 4th April 1654.
Wit. Richard Colman   signed John Catlet
     Ralph Rowze   Rec. 10th April 1654.

p.83.   Letter from John Catlet to "Mr Taylor". "my love to you and your
wife." Regarding entering the above patent for Page and Handley. Then "I
was requested by Tho Harwood to desire you in his name as the attorney of
Mrs Eaton to deliver her right in Court of the enclosed pattent to my use
& in regard I cannot be there desire some body (as Mr Gilson) to receive
it for me x x." Dated April 4th 1654.

p. 83.   August 18th 1654. "Names published to depart the colony this
year 1654.   Mr James Williamson
                  Xper Brownrig
                  John Paine
                  Wm Clapham Senr
                  Edwd Boswell
                  Hen Nicholls
                  Rich Boole
                  John Sherlock   "

p. 83.   Grant by Sr Wm Berkeley to George Eaton, 304 acres in the freshes
upon the southside of Rapa River, bordering on land of John Catlet, Ralph
Rowze and George Averye. Dated 18th June 1651.

p. 84.   Power of Atty to Tho Harwood from Mrs Joan Eaton to dispose of
estate of her son Geo Eaton, decd., for her benefit. Dated 13 Mar 1653/4.
Wit.   John Hunt
       Wm (W) Charington his mark   Recorded 18th Aug.1654.

p.84.   "Account of what sums of tobo Hen Dedman have disbursed for the
use of Antho Neesham decd.
       pd to Doctor Waldron   400
       pd for a suit of cloaths   150
       pd for a Jacket   50
       pd for a Wastecoat   25
       pd for 3 pr shoes @ 30 ppc   90
         x x x x
       pd for 2 - - to Mrs Marsh   25
       pd to Mr Bagnoll   14
       pd to Henry at Mr Jackmans for work   40
       pd to Jno Bell 1 1/2 bbl corn   150
                                            - - - - - -
                         Total   2652
           signed   Mark H.D. of
                         Hen Dodman
                 Rec. 10 Apl 1654.
Inventory of the estate of Anth Neesham, Total 1900 Tobacco.

p. 85.   Power of Atty. Nich Haile of the County of York in Virginia, planter to Tho Roots of Virga, surgeon. Dated 16th May 1654.
Wit.   John Richards   signed   Nich (NH) Haile
       Fra Butler   his mark
                             Rec. 10 June 1654.

p.86.   Bill of sale, Nicho Haile of York Co to Tho Roots of the county of Lanor, Chirurgeon, cattle and hogs.
Wit.   Fra Butler   signed   The marke N.H. of
       John Richards   Nicho Haile
                             Rec. 10 June 1654.

p. 87.   Noncup. will of Mr Tho Crowder, who departed this Life the 28th of January 1653 (1653/4) about 2 A.M. Desired Capt. John Whittey, Commander of the ship Rich & Benjamin to dispose of goods. Refers to Tho Chatwood, mercht, Tho Chewers, chururgeon, Robt Osborne, carpenter, and Wm Moulte, planter in Virginia. Directs that goods be devided betw bro. and sister's children in England.
Wit.   Tho Chatwood   Sworn before Jo Carter
       Tho Chivers
       Robt Osborne
       Wm Moult   Rec. 26th May 1654.

p.87.   Grant from Ri Bennett to Abra Moone, 300 acres bordering on land of Sir Henry Chicheley and land now in posession of Tho Kid.
Dated "19 8ber 1653."

p.88.   Assignment of above from Abra Moone to Arth Dun. Dated 8 Mar 1653.
Wit.   John Walker   signed   Abra Moone
       Bartram Hobart.

p.88.   Evan Davies and Hen Nicholls of Lanc Co. planters, sell to "Tho Wms in the county aforsd", 100 acres on S side of Rappa, on Sunderland Creek, adj. land of Rich White, John Wealsh and Mr Willis. D 5th Aug.1654.
Wit.   Rowl Burnham   signed   His mark
       Daniell Welch his mark.   Evan (E) Davies
                                                 His mark
                                          hen (N) Nicholls
                             Rec. 10th Aug. 1654.

p. 89.   Francis Batt records ownership of heifer.
                          10th August 1654.

p.89. Grant by Ri Bennett, Esq., "in the name of the Keepers of the
Liberties of England by authority of Parliament with the consent of the
Councill of State" to John Phillips, 200 acres on S. side of Rappa, on
S. side of creek known "by the name of Burnhams or Sunderland Creek" lying
at the head of a dividend of 200 acres now in posession of Edward
Boswell, bounded on N. by land of Evan Davies and Dennis Coniers, etc.
Dated "2 day of 7ber 1652."

p.90. Above assigned by Jno Phillips to Edwd Boswell 10th June 1653.
Wit. Tho Hardinge   signed   Jno Phillips
     the mark of Wm Thomas
(note: This mark, shown on the record, as many of the others are, is made
like a W upside down with short ends, thus forming a T.)
                              Rec 10th June 1654.

p. 90. "I Mathew Welbeloved do confess that it was my own voluntary
desire to be put of unto Anth Doney my now master by Mr Conawaye & that
the said Conawaye ever told me that according to his promise to my
mother he would never put me of to any man what so ever except I should
much desire it wch now I confess was my sole desire & there is not any
fault to be put into him the sd Mr Conaway In witnes that this is truth
I have hereunto set my hand this 23d day of March 1651
Witness Anth Doney   signed Mathow Welbeloved
         Enock Hauker
                         recordat 10 die Augustis 1654 "

Note: The above is to me the most interesting item in Record Book #2.
Down through the years Matthew speaks very well for his mother, for
Anthony Doney, Enock Hawker and particularly for his friend Edwin Conway.
He appears to have been taught to write, at least his name, a qualification
not posessed by all of his associates. Perhaps here we see another indica-
tion of the influence of the Eltonhead ladies. Beverley Fleet.

p.91. Deed. Dennis Coniers of Lanc. Co., planter, to Evan Davies and
Hen Nicolls, both of Lanc. Co., planters. 194 acres patented 30th March
1653, by Conyers, bordering land of Edwd Boswell, Evan Davies and Hen
Nicholls. Dated 18th March 1653/4.
No witnesses shown.   signed   Denis Coniers
                                           Ambrose Tindall
                           Recorded 10th June 1654.

p. 91. Patent issued by Ri Bennett to Tho Wilkinson. 320 acres about two
miles from the land of Rich Colman and bounded by land of Tho Lucas.
Date omitted in record.

p. 92. Tho above sold by Tho Wilkinson to Tho Lucas 5th Dec 1653.
Wit. James Butt   signed   the mark of
     Edw Myhill   Tho Wilkinson
(Note: The name above which I assume to be Lucas is very difficult to
read. It may be Luias or Lujas. B.F.)

24

p. 92. Power of Atty Tho Wilkinson of Rapa. Lanc Co., to Mr Richard
Perrot of Rapa., to deliver to Tho Lucas his right in 320 acres.
Dated "24th 9ber 1653.   signed   The mark of
Wit. John Catlett   Tho Wilkinson
      Thomas Hauking   Recorded 10th June 1654.

p.93. Grant Sr. Wm. Berkeley to Jno Nicholls 200 acres abutting upon
land of Wm Clapham on Corotoman River. Dated "3d 7ber 1651.

p. 93. Jno Nicholls assigns above land to Robt Perfet 20th Feb 1653/4.
Wit. Howell Powell   signed   Jno Nicholls
      Thomas Powell   Recorded 10th June 1654.

p. 94. "Charles Kinge of the County of Lancaster do ingage & bind myself
x x to pay unto Tho Perfect son of Robt Perfect lately decd one cow calf
x x x which calf with her increase shall remain for the use of Tho Perfect
& his heirs and assigns forever given him freely by John Meridith of the
same county x x x for as much as Robt Perfect was indebted to John
Meredith 259 lb of tobo the said John Meredith in lieu of the sd tobo hath
accepted of the said calf & freely given it to the sd Tho Perfect."
Dated 6th day of June 1654.   signed Charles Kinge
Wit. Howell Powell
      Vin Stanford   Recorded 10th June 1654.

(Note: Bully for John & Charley ! B.F.)

p. 94."Nich Haile of the Back river in the county of York" sells to "Enock
Hauker of the County of Rapa" a heifer. Dated "5th 7ber 1653".
Wit Fra Butler   signed The mark (NH) of
     Tho Burrough   Nich Haile

p. 94. Enock Hauker of Lanc. Co gives to Enock Doney the above heifer.
Dated 28th March 1654.   signed Enock Hauker
Wit Tho Roots   Recorded 19th May 1654.

p. 95. Enock Hauker gives to Charles Doney a heifer 3 yrs old of a brown
color etc. No signature or witnesses shown on record.
                          Recorded 19th May 1654.

p. 95. Grant Ri Bennett to Wm Jonson 176 acres bordering on land of Mr.
jno Cox, "the land wher sd Wm Jonson now liveth." Dated 10th Mar 1653/4.

p. 95. The above land assigned to Paul Brewer by Will Jonson 11 Aug 1654
Wit James Williamson   signed   Will Jonson
                        Recorded "10th 8bris 1654"

p. 96. Inventory of Est. of Robt Chambers, April 10th 1654 Total 4372.
Appraised by Richard Lawson and Rich Colman.

Debts due the estate from	Tob & C.
John Rogers of Chickacowan	640
More is Dr a/c a steer of 2 years old	300
James Pascall 2 bills one of	734
one of	376
	- - - -
	2050

James Peris Bond for L 30 sterl
Peter Garlands bill of sale for a quarter part of a barque
Refers to John Weir

Rec. "10th 'bris 1654.

p.96. Inventory of Est. of John Taylor, decd., appraised 2nd 8ber 1654.
Includes "3 old bibles & 2 other English books   70
Total val. 9590 tobo.   signed   Hugh Brent
Prob. a/c Toby Horton & Eliz uxor.   Teage (F) Floyne
                        Rec. "10 8bris 1654."

p.98.   Tho Paine and Penelope Paine his wife sell to Wm Hall, Wm Savage
and Wm Lenell, 300 acres in Lanc Co. on S. side of Rappa, originally
patented 7th Jan 1652/3 by Thos Paine. Dated 10th April 1654.
Wit. Mynor (M) Minson   signed   Thomas (TP) Paine
        the mark   his mark
    Abra Moone   Penelope Paine
                    Rec. "10 8bris 1654."
    "This deed if any part thereof should happen to fall into any Land
that I may claim I do hereby fully grant unto the above mentioned Tho
Paine & his assigns herein mentioned witness my hand & seal this 10th
day of April 1654   signed   Toby Smith"
                    Rec. "10 8bris 1654."

p. 99. Deed Will Jonson to Rich Kinge and Hen Bore (Bere ?) 100 acres
bordering on land of Robt Young. Dated 18 Aug 1654.
Wit. Hen Dent   signed   Will Jonson
        Anth Jackman his mark   Rec. "10 8bris 1654."

p.99. Matthews Humphreys records a calf for Wm the son of Wm Nicholls
                    Rec. "10 8bris 1654."

p.99. "A true acoct of Cattle given in by Rice Jones belonging to the
children of Sampson Wms." 3 cows, 2 heifers and 2 cow calves "joyntly
between the three children two cows & one cow calf belonging to Elizab
Wms the youngest being the produce of a gift given formerly by Mr
Paternoster decd."   signed   His
                              Rice (R E) Jones
                                    mark.
        Rec. "6 8bris 1654."

p.99. "The Estate of the orphans of Tho Dale decd vizt Tho Dale hath 800 acres of Land in Rapa river in the County of Lancaster 7 cows and 2 heifers 2 years old next March and five calves Sara Dale orphan hath 2 cows & 1 heifer of 2 years old next March & 1 cow calf Given in by Richard Perrot that married the widdow Dale."

Rec. "6 8bris 1654."

p.100. Grant by Ri Bennett to Da Welsh 537 acres in Lanc, on S. side of Rapa River and on N. side Sunderland Creek, bordering land of Rich Lewis. Dated 9th Aug 1652.   Rec. 15th Aug 1654.

p.100. Dan Welsh assigns above to Wm Caplan, Carpenter, 6th Aug.1654.
Wit. Abra Weekes   signed   His
      Robt Taylor   Dan (O) Welch
                                       mark

Rec. 15th Aug 1654.

p.100. Da Welch planter to Wm Copland, carpenter. 28th March 1655.
Wit Wm Brinker
     The mark of Evan Davies.

p.101. Deed. Walter Herd, planter, of Lanc Co. to John Meredith, shipwright, of Co of Lanc., 300 acres left Meredith by Elyas Edmonds, decd., on north side of Eastern branch of Corotoman River. Dated 6th Aug. 1654.   signed Walt (mark) Herd.
Wit Howell Powell
     Thomas Powell
     Tho (mark) Hopkins   Rec-date not shown.

p. 102. Power of Atty from Tho Chettwood of London, merchant to "Mr Peter Knight of Wiccowmoco in the County of Nothumberland" to collect debts. Dated 8th May 1655.   signed   Tho Chetwood
Wit. Geo Dobson
     John Harris   Rec. date not shown.

p.102. Inventory of Est. of Wm Ireland. All personal items. Total 199 tob.
                       signed   Tho Pettitt
                             Clemnell Trush   (Clement)
"The praisers of this Estate hath been deposed before me   Andrew Jellson"
Rec. 6th June 1655.

Note: The rather choice item to follow, unfortunately seems to have come to a dead end in the following generation. The boy seems to have had his name changed to Parrott and to have d.s.p. Richard Perrot undoubtedly was a responsible person and so was Margaret Dedman from the standards of her time and perhaps of our own. Within five years to follow came Charles 11-this English King who set our colonials such a remarkable example in having 16 children. B.F.

p. 102.   "Know all men by these presents that I Rich Perrott of Rapa do acknowledge my self to stand indebted to Margaret Dedman spinster for the use of Henry Dedman son to the sd Margaret one hundred pounds sterl mony of England woh is for a valuable consideration in hand recd this mony to be pd to the sd Henry at his age of one and twenty years In witnes to the truth hereof I have hereunto set my hand & seale this 28th day of April 1655

The considtcon of this obligation is such that if the above sd Parrott shall not provide for the above sd Henry in furnishing all manner of necessarys & provide for the bringing of him up in learning till such a time as he comes of age that then the above sd sum of mony be present pd down upon such default made to the sd Margaret to be put out to use for the maintenance of the said child But if the sd Parrott shall prove for the sd child as above sd til he come of age & after he is at age to make his estate equal with the estate of any of his own children then this bond to be void and of none effect but otherwise to be of full force and virtue and to the true performance hereof I hereby bind myself my heirs Exors & assigns In witnes whereof he hath herein to Interchangeably set his hand & seale this 28th of April 1655

Teste   signed   Richard Perrott
William Underwood
the mark RI of Rice Jones   recognit 6 Junij et recordat 25 et in
                                  anno 1655"

p. 103.   Elinor Harrison widow bequeaths, after her decease all her goods to her children. (not named)   22 Sept 1652.
Wit. William Wright   signed Elinor Harrison
      George Burch   her (EE) mark
                            Rec: 20 June 1655.

p.103.   Abraham Moone for consideration received from Tho Greefith sells 500 acres to Leroy Greefith the son of Thomas Greefieth on the freshes of Rappa. River. Dated "the 21st 1655" (sic)
Wit. James Bagnell   signed   Abra Moune
      John Phillips   "recognit 6 August et recordat 20th of
                                          anno 1655" (sic)
Note: The above name is, of course Griffin. B.F.)

p. 104.   Wm Clapham, Sr., gives "before I take my voyage for England" a cow calf to "Eliza Diemond my faithful servt". Dated 20th April 1655.
Wit. Howell Powell   signed   The mark of
      William (W) Hutchins mark   Wm (JW) Clapham
                            Rec. 20 Aug 1655.

p. 104.   Fran Place gives 300 acres and cattle to " my Daughter Mary Place" when she arrives at 18 yrs of age, she dying or failing in heirs, "to Margaret Place my youngest daughter." Dated 11th Aug. 1655.
Wit.   John Ware   signed   Fra Place his mark.
        Vin Stanford
        John Philips   Rec. 10th Nov. 1655.

p. 105.   Wm Clapham, Senr., planter, gives calf "before I take my Voiage for England" to John Makefassonn my faithful servant." D. 24 Apl.1655.
Wit.   Howell Powell   signed   The mark of
        William Hutchins his mark   William Clapham
                                 Rec. "10 9ber 1655".

p. 105. William Clapham, Senr., gives a calf to my faithful servt John Watton. (this name may be Walton or Wallon) Dated 24th April 1655.
Wit.   How Powell   signed   The mark of
        Wm Hutchins his mark.   William Clapham
                                 Rec. 10 9ber 1655.

p.106.   Walter Herd of Co. of Lanc., planter, gives cattle to "my loving brother Hen Herd". Dated 11 Aug. 1655.
Wit.   Howell Powell   signed   Walter (M) Herd
        Tho Powell   Rec. 10 November 1655.

p. 106.   John Paine, Senr., of Lanc. gives to John Pine (sic) Junr., one heifer. To his son Richard Paine one heifer. No date.
No witnesses   signed   John Paine
                                 Rec. 10 day 9ber (Nov) 1655.

p. 107.   Feb. 6th 1655/6. Deed of gift Mr Wm. Underwood to Eliza Fantleroy a cow given in 1652.
              A gift of Capt Fantleroy to Wm. Williamson, a cow given in 1653.
                              Rec. 10th Nov. 1655.

p. 107.   14 head of cattle listed belonging to the estate of Elias Edmonds, decd., per John Merridith and Vin Stanford.
                              Rec. 25th 8ber 1655.

p. 107 Refers to heifer given by Tho Harwood to Eliz dau of John Merryman.   Rec. 15th June 1656.

p. 108. Grant to J. Phillips by Richard Bennett etc, 400 acres in Lanc Co
on N. side Rapa River adj. land formerly surveyed by Capt Daniell Gookins
for transportation of 8 persons, names not shown, into the colony. Dated
13th July 1653.   Rec 12 June 1656.

Moore Fantleroy admr of Est. of Jo Phillips, decd., assigns above
patent to Vinc Stanford. Dated 2nd April 1656.
Wit. Rich Blewford   signed   M Fantleroy
     his mark   Rec. 12 June 1656.

p. 109 Moore Fantleroy admr of est of Jo Phillips, decd., sells to Vinc
Stanford 400 acres (above) and a yearling at Mr Coles upon Rapa River.
March 19 1655/6.   signed M Fantleroy
Wit Rich James.   Rec 12 June 1656.

p.109. Power of Atty. Lambert Lambethson of Lanc. Co., planter, to Mr.
John Sherlocke of Lanc. Co., to collect accounts. Dated 6th May 1656.
Wit Jo Younge his mark   signed Lambert Lambethson
    Roger Batten   Vaunder Velden
                                  Rec. 17th June 1656.

p. 110.   Thos Meather complains that Lambert Lambethson"hath privately
absented himself out of this County of Lancaster & disposed of the greater
part of his Estate". That he was bound unto Lt Coll Ellyott for 4500 lb
of tobo etc. Dated 16 May 1656.   signed John Carter
To the Sheriff of Lanc.   Rec. 16 June 1656.

June 12th x x by virtue of an attachmt under and from the
hands of Col Jo Carter dated 16th May 1656.
          In the hands of Robt Wieldie   1000 tobo
          In the hands of Wm Wright and Robt Sison 3000
          One bed and bolster and pillow and rug and a
             chest wth all that is in it all which goods
          are in the hands of Mr Thulocke
                         Teste Vinc Stanford Comr Lancaster,
                         Recorded 16th June 1656

     Petition of Tho Meather to the Commissioners of Lanc. Co. "That
your Petitioner standest engaged unto Lt Coll Ellyot in the sum of 4500
lb of tobo within one years forbearance ever since the yeare 1653 for Mr
Lambert Lambethsonx x x & the sd Lambethson having exempted himselfe out
of this river x x". Meather has counter bond etc.
                         Recorded 17th June 1656.

p. 111. Mark of Walter Herd recorded 15th April 1656.

p. 111. Power of Atty Jacob Esterbrook of London, maryner to Hum Booth
in Virginia, merchant, to collect debts. Dated 20 April 1656.
Wit. Pet Bonerey   signed the mark of Ja Esterbrook
     Jo Merideth
     Ma Hoare   No date of Rec shown.

p. 112. Francis Goare sells 280 acres to Thomas Pettit,
         Mr Andrew Gilson Mr George Taylor.
       Rec. 23rd June 1656.
   "We Thomas Williams & Alexander Porteus assign our right & title to
within specified Land to James Williamson." Dated 6th Aug. – –.
       signed Thomas Williams his mark
         Alex Porteus
       Recorded 23rd Sept 1656.
Note: The above entries are not altogether clear. B.F.

p. 112. Gift of Edward Grymes, decd., to Eliz Dudley one heifer
     and
    Gift of Thomas Sax decd., to Edward Dudley one red heifer.
      Recorded 23rd Sept 1656.

p. 113. James Bonner sells 200 acres to Patrick Miller 6th Aug. 1656.
Wit. Thomas Madestard   signed James Bonner
  John Meredith   Recorded 23rd Sept 1656.

p. 113. John Sharpe sells to Willm Tompson 300 acres on so side of Rapa
river adj land of Francis Browne now in the possession of Roger Radford.
Dated 5th May 1656.   signed John Sharpe
Wit. Thomas Warren
Elleanor Sharpe wife to John Sharpe gives consent. Rec 23 Sept 1656.

p. 114. Vine Stanford sells 300 acres formerly purchased from Thomas
Hamp (Kemp ?) and John Ashley to James Machmun and Alexander Reade.
Dated May 20th 1656.   signed Vine Stanford
Witness. Charles Hill
    Rich Davis   Rec. 23rd Sept 1656.

p. 114. " Dennys Connyers of the County of Lancaster planter have assigned
& let over unto Charles Hill of the County of Glouster cordwayner 400
acres of Land 300 lying toward the head of Pianketanck river on the North-
east side thereof beginning at a marked tree of Mrs Ellenor Brocas extending N.W. upon a line of markt trees along the line of the Land of Abraham
Moone 320 poles upon the head extending upon a swamp commonly called by
the name of the great swamp x x on the lower side of the land which the sd
Dennys Connyers now liveth upon x x toward the mouth of the river x x"
Dated May 8th 1655.   signed   The mark of
Wit. Tho Hardinge   Dennys Connyers his seale
   Erasmus Cholmley
Charles Hill assigns to Thomas Harwood the 300 acres first expressed in
above. Dated 5th August 1656.   signed Charles Hill
Wit. Philip Stevenson
   Edward Dale   Recorded 23rd Sept 1656.

p. 115. Patent Edward Digges Esq., etc. to Charles Hill 150 acres being
due f6r transporting 3 persons (names not shown) into the colony.
6th March 1655.

p. 116. Charles Hill assigns above land to Thomas Harwood with "consent
of my wife Andrew Hill" (sic) Dated 2nd April - -.
Wit Philip Stevenson   signed Charles Hill (seale)
     John Bayley   Andrew Hill her mark.
                        Recorded 23rd Sept 1656.

p. 116. Dennys Connyers of Pianketanok in the county of Lancaster
planter sells to Peter Godson 100 acres of land 15th August 1656.
"Memorandum that sd Peter is to administer Physick or Physical means to
the sd Dennys for his own person for the space of one year in part consideration of the sd Land"   signed Dennys Connyers seale
Wit. M Fantleroy   his mark
      Toby Smith
      Cuth Potter
In case Godson desires to dispose of the land Conyers to have refusal.
                        Recorded 23rd Sept 1656.

p. 117. James Hare freeman and planter of Virginia in Westmorland County
releases George Beyer of cattle and other debts.
Wit. Thomas Moulton   signed James Hare his mark
      Leonard Jones his mark
      John Younge his mark   Recorded 23rd Sept 1656.

p. 118. "Brother Lawson Let me request you to record one black heifer
x x given x x unto John Harpr son of Willm Harper (or Willm Harp Sr) of
Rappahannock x x 22 of Jan 1655 "   signed Rich Lawson
Wit Thomas Madestard   Recorded 23rd Sept 1656.

p. 118.   Thomas Best binds himself to pay to Capt More Fantleroy 4000
lb tobo. Dated 8th Jan 1655/6.   signed Tho Best
Wit Willm Mosely
     Andrew Gilson   Recorded 5 Nov. 1656.

p. 118. Coll John Carter being bound for England, makes George Marsh
"my lawful attorney". Dated 3rd June 1656.
Wit. Tho Chittwood   signed John Carter (seale)
      Jasper Baker   Recorded 5th Nov. 1656.

32

p. 119   " January 12th 1646   Memorandum
        That Capt Henry Fleet do acquit & discharge John Rosier cler (? this
word may be an abbreviation for Eldr) from all debts bills & bonds and
all other accots whatsoever from the beginning of the world unto the day
of the date hereof witnes my hand the day and year above written
                                signed   Henry Fleet
        Capt Fleet can say nothing to the contrary but that the acquits
above mentioned is his act and deed
                        record 5th die Nov 1656"

Note: John must have pledged everything on earth he had ever had including his breeches to Henry, and then after ten years become a little
nervous about the release and had it recorded. We wonder if Henry did
say anything, this writer having found it very difficult at times to cork
up creditors, even after they have been paid-if ever. B.F.

p. 119. "Know all men by these presents that I Nicholas Meriwether for
a valuable consideration already recd do sell assign make over & transfer
unto Capt Henry Fleet his heirs Exrs & assigns the full right title and
interest that I have to the within mentioned pattent warranting the sale
hereof in particular agt any by from or under me the sd Merriwether or
any by from or under me the sd Merriwether or any by from or under Colonel
Hill Witnesing my hand this 'th of September 1656
Signed & delivered   signed Nich Merywither
in the presence of
    Jo Barrow his mark   recognit in Curt 5th die No anno 1656
    Tho Wilcocks his mark   record 7 ejusdem mensis   "

p. 119   "Mr Dale
            Pray do me the favor as to acknowledge on my behalfe one
assignment of a pattent of 2000 acres unto Capt Henry Fleet and one
assignment of a pattent of 600 acres unto John Barrow let this be done
the first conveniency as Rappah Court wherein you will engage Sept the
8th 1656   Your Brother & Servt
                                Nicholas Merywether
                        recognit 5th No 1656
                        record 7 die Nov 1656 "

p. 119.   Power of Atty George Johnson of the county of York in Virginia
to his friend Thomas Willys to recover part "of my Brother John Johnsons
Estate that shall be for the good of the children." Dated 11 Dec. 1655.
Wit. John Curtys   signed   George Johnson
        Millard Turton   Rec. 12 Nov. 1656.

p. 120   Power of Atty. Willard Walthall of the county of Henrico,mercht,,
to Humphrey Booth of Rapa, merchant "to recover for me in my name and to
my use as lawful admr of Lawrence Evans mercht decd of Majr Carter who
married the relict of Capt Brocas decd the full sum of 4700 tobo due by
the said Brocas x x". Dated 26th July 1656.
Signed sealed & consigned to the   signed   Wm Walthall
above named Humphrey Booth in the
presence of   Arthur Skynner cler Curt Henr
        William Burford   record 12 Nov 1656."

Note: Col. Carter seems to have married a debt of 4700 lb of tobo as well
as one of the delightful Eltonhead ladies. B.F.

p. 121.   "Mr Williamson
          I would desire you to pay unto this bearer Thomas
Jiggells two hundred fifty & four pounds of tobo woh rests due unto me
upon accot the last year & in so doing you will engage me to remain
yours to use   signed Adam Westgate
New England this 8th of 7bor 1656
Toste Sam Pickman   record Jan 16th anno 1656."

p. 121. Letter from Tho Bries regarding suit of Robt Tomlyn.
Dated 10th Jan 1656/7.   Rec. 20 Jan 1656/7.

p. 121. Inventory of "the late decd Mr Wm Tignor". Dated 4th Feb 1656/7
Includes coopers and carpenters tools.
          "one very small warming pan   30
          one maid servt by name Alice Juxon   1200
          one new hand a man servt something ancient   1200 "
Total 14520 tobo.   signed Thomas Duncombe
                                   Peter Rigby
                                   George Kibble
                                   Thomas Madestard
    "exhibit in curt primo die Aprl 1657 a/c Mabell the relict of the sd
Willm Tignor & now wife of Willm Leech: x x " Rec. 16 Apl. 1657.

p. 122. Power of Atty to John Jefferys of London, merchant, from Wm
White of Lancaster Co., "in Rapa river in Virginia Clerk & Martha my wife
Exor of the last will & testamt of Thomas Bries of the sd county of Lanr
gent decd" to receive from Coll Robt Hooper of London, mercht., sums of
money due from sd Hooper unto afsd Thos Bries decd. Dated 25th May 1657.
Wit. Thomas Hastler   signed Willm White
      John Haslewood   Martha White
      Edmund Huddle   Rec. 25th May 1657.

p. 123. Geo Marsh of Rapa. Merchant, sells Thomas Carter 560 acres, 14th
day of Jan 1656/7.   signed Geo Marsh the seale
Wit. David Milles
      Francis Basselldin   Rec. 28th July 1657.
John Carter gives mortgage for above.

p. 123. "Whereas there is a parcel of Land at Blackwater in the Isle of
White County belonging to me Nicholas George & Thomas Taverner & Humphrey
Clerke jointly being sold for me & by the sd parties unto Francis Ayres
x x x I the sd Nicholas George my wife Margaret George & my son Nicholas
George do acknowledge the sale x x x 27 May 1657."
                          signed Nich George
                                  Margt George
                                  Nich George Junr
              Rec. 28th May 1657.

p. 124.   John Simpson of York, glasier, agrees to pay to Robt Rinsey 1500 tobo and "one anchor of dutch drams" on 10 Oct next. D 14 Mar 1657/8
Wit. Lanr Hulett   signed John Simpson
                        Rec 20 June 1657 Edw Dale Cl Curt.

Note: Always interested in a dram I cannot but wonder what on earth this can be. B.F.

p. 125.   Inventory of Thos Hackett decd., 11th Feb 1656/7.
Includes "one old Cort cupboard & an old preseit   100 tobo"
Total val 4190 tobo.   signed Nicholas George
                                          Tho Powell
                                          Howell Powell
                        Rec 20 Feb 1656/7.
a/c of Mary Hackett widdow
    to Mr Peter Knight   1600
    to Mr Nath Bacon   300
    to John Sharpe   1000
    to Mr Edw Dale for Levys   407
    to funeral charge what the Court pleaseth
    To Mr Ball   4000
                        Total 7307
                        Rec 20 Feb 1656/7.

Note: Here is an item to make an antique hunter's hair stand right on end. These things were already old in 1657-and worth 100 lb. of tobo. In 1937 worth perhaps $10,000 to $20,000.   B.F.
Note # 2: We cannot help but wonder what Yankee ruffian burned these things up in the eighteen sixties or what good Virginian split them up into fire wood to warm himself from the rear at any old time. B.F.

p. 126.   Inventory "Tho Cooper of this Co late deceased". Appr by Mr Tho Powell. Total Val. 2513 tobo.   Rec. 1 June 1658.

p. 126.   A/c of George Vezey and Nathaniel Browne upon the est of Thomas Cooper decd.
                To Mr Raleigh Travers   288
                    Mr Thos Powell   600
                    Mr Ball merone   200
                    funeral charges   500
                    the sd Vezey & Browne owing   100
                    clerks fees   234
                                              - - - - -
                                                   1922
                        Rec. 1 June 1658.

p. 127.   Inventory of Mr Thomas Prettymans personal estate, listed not valued.   signed Math Kemp
                        Exhib 9th May 1660
                        Rec   20th May 1660

See next page.

p. 127. "Account of what Debts I have pd & am obliged to pay out of Mr
Tho Prettymans personal Estate

Impr to Mr David Fox for a horse	L15. 0. 0.
To Capt Jo Whittey	5.10. 0.
To Mr Griffin admr of Mr Dixon	2. 0. 0
To Mr Griffin for a bill assigned over from	
Mr Foxcroft to Mr Dixon	4. 0. 0.
To Coll Richd Lee (sic)	1. 0. 0.
To Mr Cuth Potter	1.10. 0.
To Mr Husle	900 tobo
Wm Frizell	500
Jno Dun	400
Mr Will Ball	212
	- - - - -
	2012

Impr pd to Mr Cuthbert one cow & calf
Exhib in our 9 May 1660 by Math Kempe " Rec. 20 May 1660.

p. 128. Abraham Weekes & Robt Taylor appointed by Court to appr. Est of
Minor Minson, decd. Total val 2534 tobo. Dated April 16 1659.
            Exhib in Court per Richd Perrott and recorded 20 May.

A/c upon Minor Minsons Estate.

for his funeral charges	300
to the Doctor a/c bill	500
to Dan Johnson by bill	370
to Robt Kempe by bill	800
to John Vause by bill	180
to Mr Patteson by bill	160
to Geo Braden for his Wages Due	1000
to Capt Pensax by bill L 7 Sterl	
to Mr Travers by bill	226
to Mr Dale a/c fees	339
	- - - - -
	3875

Exhibit in our 9 May 1660 by Richard Perrot   Rec. 20 May 1660.
                                                Edward Dale cl our

p. 129.   "An acct of the Estate of Thos Dale decd x x Ten cows & heifers
the youngest 2 years old & 1 calf given to my son Richd Perrott by his
brother Thomas Dale decd A patent of 800 acres of Land that belongeth to
Rd Perrot the - - as heir to his brother Thos Dale decd."
"Exhib in our 9 May 1660 by Richd Perrot & recorded 20 May Edw Dale cl our

p. 129.   June 7th 1660. Inventory of Mr Peter Rigby decd. Total 14026.
                        signed Rowe Haddaway
                                Willm Dudley
                                John Scarbro Jur   (sic)
                                George Kibble
"Exhib in our 11 Jul 1660 a/c Tho Hill Jur " Rec 1 Aug 1660.

36

p. 130. Edward Streator of Nansemond Co., in Virginia, mercht., sells to
Edmund Lund, cattle "belonging unto my predecessor Coll Tho Burbadge
decd now going at upon my plantation in Rapa River x x one being Vizt
one red heifer with a white patch on the forehead fashionable like a
heart about the age of two years & a half old the left ear cropt & a
little peice taken out from the upper of the same ear the right ear slit
x x x." Dated 7th Sept 1657   signed Edw Streator
Wit Davy Fox
      Edward Dale "recognit in our ult die Sept 1657 record primo
                    Augusti 1657 per Edw Dale cl cur."

Note: One evidently has to go to Lancaster County to find out what is
fashionable. I, for one, never before heard that a heart was. B.F.

p. 131 Glasbeck Frizell assigns land to Walter Dickeson 30th December
1657 (sic)   signed Glasbeck Frizell
Wit. Howell Powell
"recognit in Cur ultimo die Sept anno 1657 record septimo die Oct 1657"
(there seems to be some confusion here in regard to the dates B.F.)

p. 131. Roger Radford sells to Nicholas Cooke 1/2 of 300 acres "held
by virtue of a Pattent dated the first of January anno 1652 granted to
Francis Brown." Dated 20 January 1657/8.
Wit. Barth Curtys   signed   Roger Radford
                         Rec. 1 Oct 1657. (sic)

p. 132. Thos Harwood assigns to Wm Bwer (Brewer ?, Biver ?, Bmer ?)
and John Woortham bill of sale. Dated 30 Sept 1657, Recorded 7 Oct 1657.

p. 132. George Taylor of Rappahannock, Gent., sells to Mr Willm
Clappam of same, 530 acres. Dated 11 Jan 1652/3.
Wit John Philips   signed   Geo Taylor
      Tho Bries
"Recd of Willm Clappam Senr tobo due on above for Geo Taylor"
                         signed   Hum Booth.
                    Rec 7 Oct 1657.

p. 133. John Nichols binds himself to pay to Willm Clappam Senr 330
lb tobo on 10th Oct after date. Dated 30 Nov. 1653.
Wit. Tho Harding   signed John Nichols
      De Therriott   Rec. 7 Oct 1657.

      John Nichols binds himself to pay to Willm Clappam Senr 1823
lb tobo on 10th of Oct. next ensuing. Dated 1 April 1654.
Wit. Thomas Harding   signed   John Nichols
      Martha Harding   Rec. 7 Oct 1657.

p. 133. Jno Nichols binds himself to pay Capt Thos Hackett 2000 lb
tobo 10th Oct 1655.   signed   Jno Nichols
Wit. Tho Madestard
      Jo Millisunt
Thos Hackett assigns the above to Wm Clappam Senr with Jno Nichols
consent. 27 Oct - -.   signed   Thomas Hackett
Wit. Rich Harrold   Rec 7th Oct 1657.

p. 134. This entry is difficult to read. It appears to be a patent from
Richard Bennett 19th Oct 1653 to Patrick Miller. Land bordering that of
George Waddings.

        Patrick Miller sells above to Robert Wòlverton 20 Jan 1656/7
Wit. John Bell   signed Patrick Miller
      Rich Hacker
      Charles Hill   Rec. 7th Oct 1657.

        The above name appears as Robt Wilbertun in an agreement to seat
this land. 20th Jan 1656/7.   signed Robt Wilburton
Wit   John Bell   Rec. 7th Oct 1657.

p. 135.   Tho Powell gives to Howell Powell 400 acres patented by him on
Corotoman River. 17th Sept 1657.   signed Tho Powell
Wit. Richard Gorsuch
      Jiremy Clarke
Anne Powell wife of Tho Powell agrees to the above. Rec 7 Oct 1657.

p. 135. Power of Atty from Samuell Pensax of London, mariner, to Miles
Dixon in Va., merchant. Dated 29th May 1657.
Wit. Peter Bonery   signed Sam Pensax
      John Pensax   Rec. - - Nov. 1657.

p. 136. Jno Phillips acks. himself indebted to Capt Daniell How 300 lb
tobo payable 10th Nov. next. Dated 20 May 1653.
Wit Tho Hardinge   signed   Jo Philips
     James Butt   Rec. 5 Nov. 1657.

p. 136. Bill binding Daniell Johnson to pay Willm Clappam Junr 356 lb
tobo 10th Oct. next. Dated 17 May 1653
Wit Tho Madestard   signed Daniell Johnson
    Francis Brown   Rec. 15 Nov 1657.

p. 137. Willm Clappam Junr forgives Capt Daniell How specified bill.
Dated 13 May 1653   signed   Will Clappam jr
Wit Tho Madestard
    Peter Garland   Rec 15th Nov 1657.

p. 137.   Bill binding John Edgecombe to pay to Daniell How 402 lb tobo
10th Nov. next. Dated 3 May 1653.   signed   John Edgecombe
Wit.   Peter Garland
        James Bagnoll   Rec 15 Nov 1657.

p. 137.   Toby Smith binds himself to pay 295 lb tobo before 10th Nov next
to Thos Besson. Dated 19th May 1649.   signed   Toby Smith
Wit M Fantleroy   Rec 15 Nov 1657
"Mr Smith pray upon sight hereof pay this bill to Mr John Lord or his
order for the use of your friend
10 June 1657   signed   Tho Besson"

p. 137.   Mr David Fox binds himself to pay Capt Daniell How 291 lb tobo
10th Nov. next. Dated May 22 1653.   signed David Fox
Wit.   Nich Ferman   Rec 15 Nov. 1657.

p. 137.   Willm Clappam Junr binds himself to pay Capt Daniell How 155 lb
tobo 10th Nov next. Dated May 7th 1653. signed   Will Clappam Jr
Wit.   Peter Garland
        Thom Madestard   Rec 15 Nov. 1657.

p. 138.   John Meredith binds himself to pay 1246 lb tobo to Daniell How
10th Nov. next. Dated 6th May 1653.   signed   John Meredith
Wit.   John Philips
        Peter Garland   Rec 15th Nov 1657.

p. 138.   Bill binding Will Underwood to pay Capt Daniell How 760 lb tobo.
Dated 5th May 1653.   signed   Will Underwood
Wit James Will
     John Richardson   Rec 15 Nov. 1657.

p. 138.   Bill of Will Clappam, Senr to pay to Eppey Boney 330 lb tobo in
Corotoman River 10th Nov. next. Dated 30 April 1654.
Wit.   John Philips   signed   Willm Clapham sen
        Vincent Stanford   Rec 15 Nov 1657.
" I assign all my right title of this within mentioned bill unto Capt
Hen Fleet or his asss as witnes my hand this 10th of July 1654
Wit Will Moseley   signed   Eppey Bonnison "

p. 138.   Rowland Lawson binds himself to pay to George Abbott, mercht,
250 lb tobo 1st Nov next. Dated 12th Feb 1648/9
Wit.   Epa Lawson   signed   Rowland Lawson
                        Rec. 15th Nov 1657.

p. 138.   Willm Harpr binds himself to pay Giles Webb 144 lb tobo "to be paid at Mr Lawsons dwelling house by the first of October next."
Dated 29th May 1648   signed Willm Harpr
Wit. Robert Small   Reo 15 Nov 1657

p. 139.   Enock Hawker binds himself to pay Mr Edmund Scarborough mercht, 300 lb tobo 10th Oot next. Dated 23 May 1653. signed Enock Hawker
Wit Robert Pitt   Rec 15 Nov 1657.

p. 139.   Willm Clappam (sic) binds himself to pay Edmond Scarborough 324 lb tobo 10th Nov. next. Dated 23 May 1653.
Wit. John Vines   signed WC
       Robt Pitt   Rec. 15 Nov. 1657.

p.139.   Thos Bourne binds himself to pay Edmund Scarborough mercht 180 lbs tobe 10th Oct next. Dated 25th May 1653. signed Tho Bourne
Wit. Robt Pitt   No date of record shown.

p. 139.   John Smither binds himself to pay Mr Edmond Scarborough mercht 55 lb tobo "in the river of Pianketanck" on demand. Dated 10 May 1653.
Wit. Robt Pitt   signed John Smither
                                   Rec. 15th Nov.1657.

p. 140.   Thomas Williams "according to act of Assembly 10 Nov 1657" registers mark on cattle.   Rec 15 Nov 1657 per Edw Dale ol curt

p. 140 "Certificate to James Towne a/c tre (sic) to Mr Brereton
memorandum   That I John Nichols of Lancaster do owe x x John Carter 3059 lb tobo to be pd Oct next". Dated 12th March 1654.
Wit. Charles Kinge   signed John Nichols
       Richard Flower   Rec 15 Nov 1657.

p. 140.   John Meredith and Will Clapham Junr bind themselves to hold Mr George Marsh harmless from claims of Coll Sam Matthews to 560 acres patented 10th Oct 1652. Dated 1 April 1654.
Wit. Thos Madestard   signed   John Meredith
       Will Hutchins   Will Clappam Junr.
                                   Rec 15th Nov. 1657.

p. 140. John Meredith of Corotoman River binds himself to pay to "Robert Henfield Commander of the Mary" 707 lb tobo upon demand in Corotoman River. Dated 16th Feb 1654. signed John Meredith
Wit. John Vines
Thomas Tucker   Rec. 15th Nov 1657.

p. 141. "The agreement made x x at the house of Mr Henry Corbyn on the seventeenth day of November 1657 between Samuel Cole Clerk & the major part of the Inhabitants of the parish of Lancaster in Rapa River x x that the sd Samuel Cole doth promise x x to serve them in the office x x of minister every other Sabbath so long as he shall remain in this colony
     That he will fulfil x x all Christenings burials marriages Churchings & what else is proper to his office x x x x It is agreed x x by the sd Samuel Cole & the major part of the Inhabitants now met together that a Church shall be built with all convenient speed on Mr Boswells point & that the vestry now made choice of shall take care for the effecting of the same
     Lastly it is agreedx x to pay unto the sd Sam Cole the full sum of four thousand pounds of good tobo in cask yearly x x & to contribute & agree with the Inhabitants of Piankotank for the setling of a glebe & buying of a horse for the sd Mr Coles better conviency to officiate & serve both par'shs of Lanr & Piankotank x x x
                signed Samuell Cole Clerk
Samuell Cole & those under written chosen for Vestrymen for Lanor par'sh

Peter Montague	Tho Willys
Fran Cole	Edward Boswell
Richd Perrott	John Curtys
Hen Corbyn	Robt Chonninge
Cuthbert Potter	Miles Dixon
Abraham Weeks	Robert Taylor

Richd Perrot
Edward Boswell Churchwardens

Fra Cole
Tho Willys Sidesmen

                    record 15 Decem 1657
                    Edwd Dale Cl Curt   "

p. 142. Sam Gooch of Lanc planter, sells to Thos Roots of the same Co., 100 acres on Cheesemans Creek in Co. of York, which Thomas Attowell gave by will unto his eldest daughter "Mary my wife decd" for 5000 lb tobo. Dated 26th Oct 1657. signed Sam Gooch
Wit Herbert Whitfield
John Flower   Rec. 1st Jan 1657/8.

p. 143. Henry Rey binds himself to pay Minor Doodes 384 lbs tobo in Corotoman River or elsewhere in Rappahannock on 10th Oct. 1658. Dated 10th Dec 1657. signed Hen Rey
Wit. Edward Clark
George Innerey   Rec 1st Jan 1657/8.

p. 143.   James Gates of Lancr planter sells to Minor Doodes "of the
county of Nansemond mariner" 200 acres on the N. side of Rapa River adj.
land of Jno Philips, and land of Thos Cooper, patented by Gates 28 Nov
1654.   Dated 14 Jan 1655.   signed   Ja Gates
Wit.   Tho Evans   Sara Gates
       Edward Clarke
       Hendrich Lucas
Sarah Gates gives consent to "what I and my husband have set our hands"
Dated 15th Dec 1657.   signed   Sarah Gates
                          Rec. 1st Jan 1657/8.

p. 144.   " Know all men by these presents that we Will Clappam junr of
Rapa River in Virginia planter & Elizabeth Clapham my wife do ack to have
sold & recd satisfaction for 700 acres of Land according to a pattent of
Mr Epaphroditus Lawsons (upon which we now live) accept (sic) one neck of
Land sold to Mr Stephens as by his conveyance will appear & a lease made
to Capt Henry Fleet wch the sd Henry Corbyn (sic) his heirs & assgs is to
injoy the reversion of and we do oblige ourselves our heirs Exrs & Admrs
to suffer no wilfull waste to be made of any of the housing or orchards
also sold to the sd Henry nor to remove anything off the sd plantation
which according to Law ought to be continued upon the plantation and to
build one substantial tobacco house containing sixty foot in length & 12
foot pitch with sheds the sd Corbyn finding nailes when demanded & we do
oblige ourselves x x x upon demand to make to the said Henry Corbyn x x
all such deed or deeds as shall be authintick in Law for the security of
the said Land to the sd Henry x x (Vizt) if the sd Land or any part
thereof shall be at any time recovered from the sd Henry x x that then we
oblige ourselves x x to repay again so much proportionably as the said
Henry pd for it to the sd Henry or his assgs upon demand & to depart the
said Land with all that belongs to me at or upon the twentieth day of
December in the year of our Lord 1658 & that the sd Henry shall have
liberty to do what he shall think meet for the repairing of sd tobacco
houses the deeds above expressed are to be made according to those causes
and conditions witnes our hands & seales this 6th day of December 1657
                    signed   Will Clapham his mark
                             Eliz Clapham her mark
In the presence of
       George Marsh   Recognit 16 Dec 1657
       Jo Meredith   Record 1 Jan 1657/8 Edward Dale Cl Cur. "

Note: We wonder just exactly what Mr. Dale thought of this mess when he
came to record it. Whenever the rich Mr. Corbin had business to transact
with his friends the honest Clappams, it is quite evident that he availed
himself of their good old Virginia hospitality before he sat down to
write. On this occasion he seems to have forgotten whether he was himself
or Henry Fleet, which is perfectly O.K. with the writer-being descended
from both.   Beverley Fleet.

p. 145. Sam Pensax certifies that he has paid to Thomas Booth of London
8 pounds & 10 shillings on a/c of Mr John Rose in Virginia, etc.
Dated 17th April 1657.   signed Sam Pensax
                          Rec. 27th Jan 1657/8.

p. 145.   "Mr John Morcoross
            I do desire you to make an end of the difference between Mr
Fox Mr Ball and myselfe about 1000 lb of tobo & ca due unto me & do hereby
give you as full power to end the same as I have if I were present to end
the same & do hereby oblige myself to stand to abide by what end you shall
make therein & shall rest Jan 20 1657
Wit.   Tho Humphreys   Your loveing friend
        Tho Bushrode   the mark of
                                                  John Fleete
                        Rec 21st Jan 1657/8.

p. 145.   "I Henry Rye do freely give unto my son in Law Will Rogers a
brown cow and a cow calf x x the male of the breed to my selfe & the
female to the boy til he comes to fourteen years of age"
No date. No Wit.   signed   Hen Rye his mark
                        Rec 1st Feb 1657/8.

p. 145.   Grant from Edward Digges Esq.; etc., to Will Thatcher 400 acres
on N.W. side of Corotoman River bordering land of Henry Davy and land
formerly surveyed for Jno Nichols called now Perfect his land, land of
one Hull bought of one Hawker. 300 acres of this land formerly granted
the sd Will Thatcher by a patent dated 17th May 1655 and 100 acres by a/c
of transportation of 2 persons (names not shown) into colony. Dated at
James City the last day of November 1656.
                        signed   Edward Diggs
                                  Wm Claybourne, Sec.

p. 146.   "I Willm Thatcher assigns over to John Edwards 200 acres of Land
from this patent." Dated 27 Jan 1657/8.
Wit.   Tho Chettwode   signed   Will Thatcher
        Vine Stanford   Rec. 20th Feb. 1657/8.

p. 146.   Grant from Edward Diggs, etc., to Enock Hawker and Anthony Doney
1000 acres on N.W. branch of Corotoman River bounded by land of John
Nicholls. The sd land being formerly granted to sd Enock Hawker & Anthony
Doney by patent dated 6th Oct 1656.

p. 147.   Enock Hawker sells to John Walker & Willm Que land in foregoing
patent. Dated 2 Dec. 1657.   signed Enock Hawker
Wit.   Tho Chetwode
        Edward Dale
Mary Hawker consents to above.   Rec. 20 Feb 1657/8.

p. 147.   John Curtys of Lanc leases to Thos Tuggle of Lanc. 100 acres
bordering land granted to Abraham Moone. Dated 4th Jan 1657/8.
Wit.   Robt Osborne   signed   John Curtys
        Wm Morgan   Tho Tuggle
                        Rec 20 Feb 1657/8.

p. 148.   John Curtys binds himself to pay Mr David Fox 2391 lb tobo in
Rapa river Nov. 10th next. For security "one gray mare which was formerly
bought of Squire Digges by Abraham Moone x x". Dated 9th Feb 1657/8.
Wit Edm Lund   signed John Curtys
     Tho Daniell   Rec 30th May 1658.

p. 148.   Edmond Kempe of Piankotank in the county of Lancaster in Va.,
gent., binds himself to pay Isaac Foxcrofe of London, gent., 200 pounds
sterilin, the last of Nov. 1658. Dated 13th April 1658.
    " The condition of this obligation is such that if the above boundin
Edw Kempe his heirs Adms or Assns do pay or cause to be paid unto Isaac
Foxcrofe his heirs Admrs or assns the sum of one hundred pounds Storl to
be paid at the now dwelling house of Mr Thomas Griffith scituated in
St Nicholas Lane London upon the day & year of our Lord as above specified
or else to remain in full force x x"   signed Edm Kempe
Wit. Miles Dixon
     Matt Kemp   Rec 15 May 1658

p. 149.   London 9 July 1656.   Sr. Hen Chichely, Kt., is indebted to Tho
Cornwallys, Esq., 1543 lb. tobo. to be paid at "my plantation in Rapa
Virginia on the tenth day of Jan next". "in full satisfaction of a brown
bay horse delivered to Mr Cuthbert Fennicke in Virginia."
Wit John Jeffryes   signed Hen Chicheley
     Tho Colclough   Rec. 12 May 1658.

p. 149. Willm Thompson of Rapa in Lanc sells to John Jadwyn 150 acres
part of land granted John Sharpe now in possession of Willm Tomson.
Dated Dec. 3rd 1657   signed Willm Thompson
Wit Peter Montague
     Thom Warricke   Rec. 28th May 1658.

p. 150.   Thos Roots of Corotoman River gives to "my loving godson Thomas
Baughton one cow calf x x ". "x x in case the sd Tho Boughton dying
without issue then the sd calfe x x x to the father of the sd child."
Date 26th May 1658.   signed Tho Roots
No Wit.   Rec. 1st June 1658.

p. 150. Mr Rowland Burnham decd., late of Rapa in the Co of Lanc., sold
to Robt Middleton "one red cow x x reed satisfaction for the sd cow know
ye that Henry Corbyn who married the relict of the said Mr Burnham do by
these presents assign over the said Cow to the sd Robert Middleton x x "
Dated April 5th 1658.   signed Hen Corbyn
Wit. Jo Vause.
    Robt Middleton assigns right to above cow to Willm Pew. 17 Apl 1658.
Wit. Tho Willys   signed Robt Middleton
                          Rec. 1st June 1658.
    Willm Pew assigns right to above cow to Hen Nicholas. 17 Apl. 1658
Wit. Tho Willys   signed Willm Pew
                          Rec 1st June 1658.

p. 151. " Coll John Carter of Rapa River in the County of Lancaster for love and affection that I bear toward my neice Eltonheade the Daughter of Edwyn Connaway" gives a heifer now at the plantation of Willm Lucas on the S. side of the Rapa river. Dated 9th April 1656.
Wit. Jasper Baker   signed   John Carter
     Foslin Delanall   Rec 1st June 1658.

Note: The above entry which seems to have been confusing to certain of our genealogists is simply explained in that Col. Carter had recently married Eleanor Eltonhead, whose former husband had been Capt. William Brocas. She being a sister of the wives of Edwin Conway, Henry Corbin, Cuthbert Fenwick of Maryland etc. B.F.

p. 151. Cuth Fennicke, Gent., "for the love I bear unto Edwyn the son of Edwyn Connaway of Corotoman in the County of Lancaster gent" gives two heifers, increase to redound to his father during his minority.
Dated 10th June - -the year is illegible but may be 1654.
Wit. Thomas Fennicke   signed Cuth Fennicke
     William Eltonhed   Rec: 1st June 1658

p. 151. Thomas Humphreys of Lanc in Va., planter , sells to Toby Horton of same Co., planter, 600 acres on the N. side of a creek which issueth into Fleets Bay "called by the name of Haddawaies Creek as by the pattent thereof more large appears." Dated 28th Jan. 1657/8.
Wit Tho Hawkins   signed Tho Humphrey
     Edward Dale   Rec 1st June 1658

p. 152. John Nicholas of Corotoman River in Lancr sells to John Porteus planter, 200 acres "whereon Nich George now liveth upon Corotoman River". This land, according to patent, assigned to Jno Nicholas by Capt. Thomas Hackett. Nicholas refers to his wife but her name does not appear.
Dated 22nd Feb. 1657/8.   signed Jo Nicholas
Wit. Edwyn Connoway
     Mar: Conaway   Rec. 1st June 1658.

p. 153. John Simpson sells to Moore Price and Thomas Maddison 600 acres which he had bought from Alexander Porteous. Dated 18th May 1658.
Wit. Brian Stott (Scott ?)   signed John Simpson
     Tho Stott (Scott ?)   Anne Simpson
                  Rec. 1st June 1658.

Note: The appearance of the brothers Stott or Scott in this neighborhood and at this period has been an interesting but not altogether satisfactory incident so far as the writer is concerned. Edwards, who wrote the original, is inclined to make a small "o" and a small "t" exactly alike. The best authorities consulted (and I have consulted the best) give me this name as Stott. My common sense, backed by reasons others may be aware of, tells me this name is Scott. The reader of the original or of these abstracts may take his choice. Beverley Fleet.

p. 153. Patent from Edwd. Digges, etc., to Alexander Porteous 600 acres (foregoing) adj. land of Lambt Lambethson and Richd Hatton, this land formerly granted to Mr David Fox 25th Nov. 1652 and by him assigned to Porteous, for transp. 12 persons into the colony. Dated Oct. 6th 1656.

p. 154. Alex Porteous guarantees title to above. Dated 18 Feb 1655. (sic)
Wit. Sam Duke   signed Alex Porteous
     Arthur Wright   Rec. 1st June 1658.

        Alexander Porteous assigns right to foregoing patent to John
Simpson.   signed Alex Porteous
Wit Brian Stott (Scott ?)
     Ja Coghill   Rec. 1st June 1658

        Power of Atty, Alexander Porteus to Mr Thomas Chetwode. 15 May 1658
Wit. Raleigh Travers   signed Alexander Porteous
     Edw Dale   Rec. 27th May 1658.

p. 154. Dominicke Therriot sells to Richard Ball a heifer. 26 May 1658.
Wit. Jo Stevens   signed D Therriot
     Tho Roots   Rec 1 June 1658.

p. 155. Eliz Clappam gives Power of Atty to Mr. Thomas Prettyman to ack sale of 700 acres to Mr. Corbyn, 27th May 1658.
Wit Tho Medestard   signed Eliz Clappam her mark
     Sarah Medestard   Rec. 29th May 1658.

p. 155. Teage Floyne gives to Richard Lawson son of Rowland Lawson one cow calfe "and the male and female of this calfe for the use of the said Jo Lawson" (sic). Dated 1658.   signed   The mark of
No. Witnesses.   Teage Floyne
                             Rec. 27th May 1658.

p. 155. George Kibble, with consent of wife Mary Kibble, sells 92 acres in Pianketank parish to Peter Rigby. 18th Jan. 1657/8.
Wit. John Curtys   signed George Kibble his mark
     John Humphreys   Mary Kibble
                             Rec. 1st June 1658.

p. 156. John Curtys admr of Abraham Moone decd sells to Leroy Griffith the son of Thomas Griffith of Lancaster, 500 acres in the freshes of the Rapa River. Dated 2nd Dec 1656.   signed John Curtys
Wit Tho Bunbury
     Will Morgan
     Reynold Johnson
     Paul Woodbridge   Rec. 1st June 1658.

p. 156. Richard Bennett, Esq., etc., grants to "Coll Richard Lee Esqr" 300 acres in Lanc. upon S. side of Rapa. River, on Machepungo Creek, adj. land of Dame Eliz. Lunsford, for transp. of 6 persons into the colony. Dated 14th Nov. 1653.

p. 157. Coll Richd Lee assigns above land to Mr Myles Dixon, merchant, and authorizes Mr. Cuthbert Potter to ack. this in Court. Mar.1 1657/8.
Wit. Anth Elliott   signed Rich Lee
     David Cant   Rec. 1 June 1658.

p. 157. Dame Elizabeth Lunsford gives "my loving friend Richard Lee" 50 acres in Rapa River, "part of land assigned me from Sam Abbott."
Dated 28th April 1656.   signed Eliza Lunsford
Wit George Reade
     Tho Ludlowe
     Miles Dixon
            The above assigned to Mr. Miles Dixon, merchant, 15th Mar.1657/8
Wit. Anth Ellyott   signed Richd Lee
      David Cant   Rec. 1st June 1658.

p. 158. Edmond Lunsford binds himself to pay Thos Carter 2761 lb tobo 10th Oct. next. Dated 25th May 1658.   signed Edmund Lunsford
Wit. Geo Reynolds
      Jo Sperman   Rec 1st Aug 1658.

p. 158. Acknowledgement of John Meredith of a red cow calf freely given unto Hannah Jones Daughter of John Jones for divers causes him thereunto moving.   signed Jo Meredith
Wit. Will Ball   recognit 28 Jul 1658 Rec 1st Aug. 1658.

p. 158. Vincent Stanford with consent of "Mary my wife" sells 400 acres formerly purchased of the Estate of Mr John Phillips, decd., to the following persons: Robert Lollard, Willm Blunkard and Willm Stevens. This land being due by patent to Jno. Phillips, decd., and assigned over by Coll. More Fantleroy, with the consent of James Cates and Sara Cates, who was the wife of Jno. Philips. Dated Feb 9th 1657/8
Wit. Thos Maddison   signed Vinc Stanford
      Jo Potter   Rec. 1st August 1658.

p. 158. Vincent Stanford sells cattle to Willm Brinker, Robert Pollard and Willm Stephens. Dated 9th Feb. 1657/8
Wit. Tho Maddison   signed Vinc Stanford
      John Potter   Rec. 1st Aug 1658.

p. 159. Richard Bridger of Lanc., with consent of his wife Jane Bridger,
sells to Thomas Pattisonn 200 acres on head of Burnhams Creek. Land
formerly purchased by "both of the aforementioned parties of one Thomas
Kidd." Dated : Last day of June 1658.   signed Rich Bridger
Wit. Margaret Jones   Jane Bridger
        Tho Jones   Rec. 1st Aug 1658.

p. 160. William Dudley of Mockjack bey (sic) sells to Henry Thatcher
2000 acres in Lanc. Co., on S. side of Rapa. River, lying on N. side of
the Great Swamp, beginning by the land of Mr. Cuthbert Potter.
Dated 20th Feb. 1657/8   signed Will Dudley
Wit. Thomas Morrys senr
        Andrew Williamson   Rec 1st Aug. 1658.

p. 160. "Edwin Connaway did give unto Walter Herd for the use of his son
Henry a black sow with all her increase now the sd sow having six lusty
shoats the sd Walter Herd having a desire to have the hogs for his own
particular use & being willing to give two Cow calves of this years fall
for the sd sow & her shoats with all their increase both male and female
unto him & his heirs forever Now Know ye that the said Edwyn Connoway do
give my free consent thereunto & do hereby desire that the said Calves
may be made over unto Henry the son of Walter Herd with all their increase both male and female unto him and his heirs forever and they to be
marked with a crop on both ears & a half moon on the upper side of the
left ear with a slit on the sd ear witnes my hand the 17th of July 1658
Wit. Nich George   signed Edwyn Connaway
        Jo Hooper   Walter Herd
                            Rec. 1st Aug. 1658.

Note: Walter having had a little brush with the fussy Mr. Conway some
four years back, is not taking any chances with this peace offering, re-
gardless of how facinated he may have been by the litter of squealing
shoats. B.F.

p. 161.   "At a Court held at James City the 10th of December 1656
                        Present
            Edward Digges Esqr Governor
        Coll Tho Peters   Coll Matthows
        Coll Will Burnard   Capt Perry
        Coll Tho Dew   Lt. Coll Walker
    Whereas it appears to this Court by the confession of Capt Will
Brocas in his Life time that Jo Jackson was his sisters son and therefore
is now the next heir in this county to the Lands which the sd Capt Brocas
died seized of It is therefore ordered that the Sheriff of Lancaster
forthwith put the said Jackson in possession of the Lands pattented by
the sd Capt Brocas deed
                        Vera Copia
                        Test Nich Merywether cl curt
record primo August 1658 per Edwd Dale cl curt   "

p. 161. Agreement betw. Mr Vincent Stanford and Mr Thomas Daniell to be
partners for 7 years in land, plantation, etc.,whereon Vincent Stanford
now lives, which he lately bought from John Robinson, 210 acres and also
600 acres lying on N. side of Willm Brunkett's land. Dated 18 Mar.1657/8.

                                    signed Vincent Stanford
                                          Ma: Stanford

Consent of Mary Stanford wife of Vincent Stanford.
Wit. Edmd Lund
     Will Stephens   Rec. 1st August 1658.
Note: The last part of the above record is very difficult to read. B.F.

p. 163. Alex Porteus of Lanc. planter sells to Benjamin Whiscombe and
Joseph Allen of London. mariners, 270 acres of land, etc. Thomas Chetwode
appointed attorney in behalf of Porteus. Dated 6th May 1658.
Wit. Edward Stalliard   signed Alex Porteus
     Edward Dale   Rec. 27th May 1658.

p. 163. Indenture regarding foregoing 270 acres. Land described as was
or now occupied by Peter Godson and bordered by land occupied by Mr
Rawleigh Travers, that of Thomas Powell, Powell's Creek, etc.

p. 163. Alex Porteus sells cattle to Whiscombe and Allen. 6th May 1658.

p. 165. Alex Porteus sells to Jos. Allen and Benj Whiscombe the following bills: John Simpson   3944 tobo.
                    Mathew Fullerton   1080
                    Thomas Pitts   1100
                    Willm Harwood   400
                    John Alexander   80
Wit. Edward Stalliard   signed Alexander Porteus
     Edward Dale   Rec. 1st Aug. 1658.

p. 165. 29th Sept. 1658. James Gates, according to act, gives notice of
an 18 ft. boat he took up adrift.

p. 166. Grant of Richd. Bennett to Willm Harper and Henry Rye of 550
acres in Lanc. C. lying to the head of Harper's Creek, near Fleet's Bay,
and extending from the eastermost side of a southern branch of the said
creek west into the woods x x x on the westermost side of White Marsh, etc.,
for the transp. of 11 persons, names not shown, into colony. 19 Nov.1653.

       Willm & Mary Harper assign their part in above to Henry Rye.
Dated 11th Sept. 1658.   signed Will Harpr
Wit. Tho Madestard   Mary Harpr
     Will Clapp (?)   Rec. 29 Sept. 1658.

       Power of Atty. Will & Mary Harper to "our Friend Mr Willm
Clappam". Dated 12th Sept 1658.   signed Will Harpr
Wit. Tho Madestard   Ma Harpr
     Sarah Madestard   Rec 29th Sept 1658

p. 167. Will Clappam, Junr., of Lanc. Co., planter states he is indebted
to Henry Corbyn, of the same Co.,gent., "the full sum of twenty and one
thousand pounds of x x tobo" and two pieces of trading cloth containing
94 yards or thereabouts, to be pd. 20th Sept. next. Dated 29th Sept 1658.
    Refers to Bill of sale dated 6th of Dec. 1657 betw. Willm Clappam
and Henry Corbyn.   signed   Will Clappam Junr
Wit. Will Ball
      Tho Madestard   Rec. 29th Sept 1658.

p. 167. Will Thomas of Lanc. planter sells to Peter Godson 50 acres on
N. side of Rapa. in Powell's Creek, being half of a dividend of land now
lived on by Will Thomas, patented 13th July 1658. Dated 29 Sept. 1658.
Wit. Charles Hill   signed   Will Thomas
      George Flower   Joane Thomas
      Dm. Therriott   Rec. 1st Oct. 1658.

p. 168. James Bonner sells to Patrick Miller 200 acres on S. side of
Rapa, adj. land of George Warren. Dated 6th Aug. 1656.
Wit. Thomas Madestard   signed ja Bonner
      John Meredith   Rec. 23rd Sept 1656.

    Above land assigned to Will Frizel. Dated 24th Nov. 1658. (sic)
Wit. Hen Pulman (or Culman)   signed James Mackmun
      Edward Dale   Rec. 1st Oct. 1658.

p. 169. Elizabeth Mackmun gives power of atty to Mr. Tho Chetwode to ack
right and title to above land sold to Willm Frizel. Dated 23 Nov.1658
Wit. John Lampart   signed Eliz Mackmun
                                 Rec. 1st Oct 1658.

p. 169. Sarah Shipp, relict of William Shipp "of the County of Lower
Norfolk admr unto my sd husband appoint my well beloved son in law Bryan
Stott (Scott ?) living in the River of Rappahannock x x attorney" to
collect debts. Dated 21 Nov. 165-.   signed Sarah Shipp
Wit. Will Smith
      Will Sherman   Rec. 1st Oct. 1658.

p. 169. Power of Atty. John Wadington of York River, mercht, to Edward
Dale to collect debts in Lancaster Co. Dated 27th Nov. 1658.
Wit. Will Snowdell   signed Jo Waddington
      Giles Nash   Rec 1st Oct 1658.

p. 169. Samuel Matthews, Esq., grants to Vincent Stanford 500 acres on
No. side in freshes of Rapa, about 6 miles above Nansemond Town, border-
ing 1000 acres surveyed for John Gillett. This being a "dividend" due
Vincent Stanford by patent dated 20th Nov 1654.   Dated 12th October 1657.
signed Sam Matthews
Wm Claybourne Sec
Memo. Vinc Stanford assigns right in above to Mr Anthony Tibboe. Mr. Edw.
Dale given power to ack. this in Court. Dated 8th Nov. 1658.
Wit.   Robt Pollard   signed Vin Stanford
        Will Stophens   Rec. 1 Oct 1658.

p. 170. Mary Stanford widow lately wife of Vincent Stanford, late decd.,
releases interest in above land to Anthony Tibboe. Dated 24th Nov. 1658.
Wit. Charles Norwood   signed Mary Stanford
      Will Lorkyn (Lockyn ?)
      "recognit in our 24 Nov 1658 et record primo Oct sequent
                       per Edwd Dale Cl Cur"   (sic)

Note: Now Mr. Dale ! This is not the first time you have done this. B.F.

p. 170-171 Same entries re. Vincent Stanford, only for 8oo acres to Anth.
Tibboe.

p. 171. Indenture, 24th November 1658, betw. Henry Corbyn of Lancaster,
gent., and Matthew Kempe of the same Co., selling 700 acres, formerly
granted to Epaphroditus Lawson, decd., now or late was occupied by Willm
Clappam, Junr., lately purchased by Hen. Corbyn from Will Clappam, excepting a part sold to John Stephens "which neck of Land is lying and being
near unto another parcel of Land part of the promises & leased for a terme
of years yet to come & unexpired unto Lt Coll Hen Fleete (and likewise
occupied and reserved unto the aforesaid Lt Coll Hen Fleete & his assigns
The aforesaid parcel of Land part of the promises & demised unto the sd
Hen Fleete for a terme of years yet to come & unexpired according to the
tenor & contents of his demise thereof " x x .
Wit. Rawleigh Travers   signed   Hen Corbyn
      Cuth Potter   recog 24 Nov 1658 rec 1 Decemb 1658.

p. 173. Hen Colepeper, planter, in the County of Lancaster, Virginia,
assigns to John Edwards, surgeon, in the same County, one cow calf. Dated
7th Dec. 1658.   signed Hen Colepeper
Wit. Leonard Cacott
      Tho Williamson
        John Edwards, surgeon, of the County of Lancaster, assigns the
above heifer to Leonard Cacott (name blurred, looks as though it had been
altered) Dated 9th December 1658.
        "Provided that the said Cacott doth not dispose of the sd heifer
until the experation of the seven years that he is to serve me the sd
Edwards"   signed   John Edwards
Wit. Edward Dale   Rec. 17th Dec. 1658.

p. 173. "This bill bindeth me Capt Henry Fleet my heirs Exr Admrs or assg to pay or cause to be paid unto John Merryman his heirs Exors Admrs or assgs the full and just sum of six barrells of sound Indian Corne to be paid at his now dwelling house at or upon or before the last of Arrill next ensuing the date hereof as witnes my hand this 21st of Septemb 1652
Test Sam Gooch   signed Henry Fleete
   record in Curt Jan the 26th 1658 per Edwd Dale Cl Cur "

p. 173. Power of Atty from Thomas Brewer of Wiccocomoco, planter, in the County of Northumberland, to John Meredith to plead "causes on my account in Court held at Rappahannock."   signed   The mark of
Wit. John Goddin   Tho Brewer
      Henry Bentley   Rec. 28th Jan 1658/9.

p. 174.   Enock Hawker of Lanc. planter, sells to George Hicson one red heifer. Dated 11th Dec. 1658   signed   Enock Hawker
Wit. Tho Roots
      Jo Dickeson   Rec. 1st March 1658.

p. 174.   Enock Hawker sells to John Dickenson one red heifer. 27th Nov. 1658.   signed Enock Hawker
Wit. William Ball
      Richard Ball   Rec. 1st March 1658/9

p. 174.   Henry Rye of Lanc., planter, sells to Eppy Bonnison of the same county, planter, 550 acres in Lancaster "on the S. side of a Creek that issueth out of Fleets Bay called x x Hadaways Creek there issueth out of sd creek a branch called Harpers Creek." Dated 30th Nov. 1658.
Wit. Hugh Brent   signed Henry Rye
      Love Johnson   Rec. 1st March 1658/9.

p. 175.   Power of Atty. Ebby Bonnison to Hugh Brent to ack sale of 350 acres to Ever Peterson. Dated 25th Jan 1658/9.
Wit. Hen Rye   signed Ebby Bonnison
     Domingno Cras   Rec 26th Jan. 1658/9.
   "and further I the sd Walter do warrant the sd sale from my selfe and the sd Ever Peterson forever unto the sd Ebby & his heirs & do authorise Majr John Carter to acknowledge this deed in Court as witnes my hand & seale this 17th of Nov 1655   signed Walter Bruce (?)
Wit. Tho Carter
      Diana Skipwith   recog 26 Jan 1658 rec 1 March 1658 "(1658/9)

p. 175.   Ebby Bonnison assigns interest in bill of sale to Ever Peterson for land. Dated 25th Jan 1658/9.   signed Ebby Bonnison
Wit. Hen Rye
      Domingno Cras   Rec. 1st Mar 1658/9.

Note: The above entries are not altogether clear to me, however the aristocratic Col. Carter and the still more elegant Skipwith must have known what they were doing. The signature shown as Bruce is difficult to read. It well may be another name. Beverley Fleet.

p. 176. Grant from Sr. Wm. Berkeley to Rice Jones, 350 acres in Rapa River, lying about 9 miles upon the N. side, upon a point of an Island called Musketoe point. Dated 18th April 1650.

p.176. Henry Rye of Lanc. planter, sells to Ebby Bonnison of Lanc., planter, 550 acres patented 15th Oct. 1653. Dated 10th Dec 1658.
Wit. Hugh Brent   signed Hen Rye
        Love Johnson   recog 26 Jan 1658   rec 1st Mar 1658 (1658/9)

p. 177. Richard Bennett releases to Epaphroditus Lawson certain property mortgaged to Symon Overzee. The date is uncertain, it appears to be 13th April 1651.   signed Ri Bennett
                                Rec. 26th Jan 1658/9.

p. 177. Agreement dated 3rd Dec. 1658, betw. Edward Boswell of Lanc., Planter, and John Vause of the same Co., planter. Partnership in plantation for 12 years. Vause to send tobo to Boswell in England to be disposed of for joint interest. "x x that sd Edw Boswell & his wife shall not go for England this year." This is a lengthy agreement covering three pages of this large record book.   signed Edward Boswell
Wit. Andrew Butchert
        Mary Butchert   recog 19 Feb 1658   rec 1 Mar 1658 (1658/9)

p. 180. Edward Boswell acknowledges himself indebted to John Vause, both of Lancaster County and planters, "500 pounds of current English money." Dated 3rd Dec. 1658.   signed Edward Boswell
Wit Andrew Butchart
        Mary Butchart   recognit 19 Feb.1658   rec 1 March 1658 (1658/9)

p. 181. Jno Vause acks. himself indebted to Edward Boswell etc. Dated 3 Dec. 1658/9.   signed Jno Vause
Wit. Andrew Butchert
        Mary Butchert   Rec. 1 Mar. 1658/9.

p. 181. John Jones of Lanc., planter, sells to "Charles Hill of the same County of Lancaster Cordwayner" 300 acres. " x x plantation I now live on." Dated "last of March 1659."   signed   Jo Jones
Wit. Edwyn Connaway
        Howell Powell   recog 30th March 1659   rec 1st Apl 1659.

p. 182. Indenture dated 25th March 1658/9 betw Andrew Boyer, late of the County of Lancaster in Rapa River in Virginia, planter, and George Flower of the same Co., planter, selling plantation "whereupon the sd Andrew Boyer lately lived."   signed Andrew Boyer
Wit. De Therricke
        Will Thatcher   recog 30 Mar 1659   rec 1st Apl 1659.

p. 183.   Whereas Thomas Brewer of the County of Northumberland,planter,
lately by a deed sold to Andrew Boyer and Willm Thatcher 500 acres, part
"of a dividend whereon the sd Brewer now liveth." Thatcher now sells to
Andrew Boyer his interest. Dated last day of July 1658.
Wit. Edwyn Connaway   signed Will Thatcher
      Rich Gorsuch   Rec 1st Apl.1659.

p. 184.   Thos Maddeson and Moore Price ack bill of sale for a house unto
John Simpson. Dated 30th March 1659.   signed Tho Maddeson
Wit. John Stott (Scott ?)
      Bryan Stott   "   Rec 1st Apl. 1659.

p. 184.   Willm Hollingsworth, mariner, being attorney for Mr Willm
Brown of Salem, "also myself" appoints "my loving friend Walter Dickenson,
planter in Corotoman in Rapa River" attorney to collect debts.
Dated 26th Feb. 1658/9.   signed Will Hollingworth
Wit. Mordecay Nicholls
      Edward Packer (Parker ?)   Rec. 30th Mar. 1659.

p. 184.   Peter Godson assigns right to bill of sale to Will Thomas and
makes James Nicholson his atty. Dated 25th Mar 1658 (1658/9)
Wit. Tho Chowne   signed Peter Godson
                                              Sara Godson
                           Rec. 1st Apl. 1659.

p. 185.   Henry Clarke of Wicocomoco in the County of Northumberland in
Virginia acknowledges receipt from Isaac Foxcroft, mercht., several bills
of sale and accounts. Also an account of L 4. Sterl. due from Mr. Tho
Brerton. Also a boat with mast, sails, oars and rudder and "x x a man
servt named Malachi Greet valued at 1000 lb of tobo". x x "also two notes
of Mrs Eliz Vaulx the one to receive of Mr Stannton commander of the white
dove & Coop & what other goods or servants are there consigned to Mr Robt
Vaulx & the other to receive of Mr Fowke fifty shills sterl due by accot
to Mr Vaulx both directed to Mr Foxcroft & by him assigned to me x x."
Also for another note of Mrs. Eliz. Vaulx, to receive of Capt. Sam.
Pensax, commander of the Nicholas & Mary, one box , consigned to Mr. Robt.
Vaulx, by Mr. Thomas Griffith, marked (here introduced in the record is a
curious mark) wherein "is saddles & Books." Dated 26th April 1659.
Wit. Willm Ball   signed   Hen Clarke
      Hugh Kinsey.   Recorded 27th April 1659.

Note: In taking an abstract of such an entry, one cannot but wish that
Mr. Dale had occasionally made use of punctuation marks, but this gentleman was quite innocent of this complexity of civilization. B.F.

p. 185. "By the Governor & Capt General of Virginia Whereas the safety
& peace of this Colony hath been much endangered by the exhorbitant and
undue practices of some men in Contempt of the late Commission for this
Government sent from his highness & the Lords of his Council There are
therefore in the name of his highness the Lord Protector x x x to take
into your safe custody the body of Colo John Carter & him safely to de-
tain or take such sufficient security that he may answer on the third
day of May next ensuing to such matters as shall be objected agt him
on the behalf of his Highness the Lord Protector before the Governor &
Council at James City hereof fail not at your peril x x" Dated 8 Apl.1659.
To the Sherif of   signed Sam Mathews
Lancaster County or
his Deputy   record primo July 1659
                                   per Edwd Dale Cl Curt

p. 186 "This is a true copy of the originall warrant by virtue of which
original warrant Mr Travers now Sherif of this County did openly declare
he did arrest the sd Colo John Carter according to the tenor of the sd
warrant and is recorded in this Court 25th Maij 1659
                              per me Edwd Dale Cl Curt "

Note: The above incident is well known to historians and genealogists.B.F.

p. 186. Whereas there was 300 acres of land held by and betw. Nicholas
Cooke and Roger Radford, decd., half of which land "being given by will
to Mary Cole by sd Radford, know therefore that I George Marsh for good
consideration of 1000 lb of tobo recd for the use of my aforesd Daughter
in Law Mary Cole " sells to Nicholas Cooke that part of land formerly
owned by Radford. Dated 9th Feb. 1658/9.   signed George Marsh
Wit. John Webb
      Domingo Madoras   recog 25 May 1659   rec 1 July 1659

p. 186. Power of Atty from Francis and Elizabeth Browne to Geo Marsh to
ack sale of 300 acres to Nich Cooke. Dated 16th May 1659.
Wit. Tho Bunbury   signed Francis Browne
     Richard Lugg   Eliz Browne
                         Rec. 25 May 1659.

p. 186. Francis Browne of Rapa., "with consent of Elizabeth my wife
confirms all my right & claim" to that 300 acres formerly sold "unto
Roger Radford unto Nicholas Cooke his heirs or his assigns" and releases
claim to sd land. Dated 15 May 1659. signed Francis Browne
Wit. George Marsh   Eliz Browne
      Tho Bunbury   Rec. 1 July 1659

p. 187. Thomas Bourne of Piankotank in the County of Lancaster sells to
Simon Morleigh and Richard Hacker of Cheesequake in the County of York a
parcel of land lying on the Piankotank River called the rich Neck, granted Bourne 16th Sept. 1651. Dated 19th April 1652.
Wit. Richd Lake   signed Tho Bourne
      John Bell   Rec. 1st July 1659.

p. 187. Richard Hacker and Mary Hacker assign their interest in the
foregoing bill of sale to John Needles. Dated 21st March 1658/9.
Wit. Richd Davys   signed Richard Hacker
      Hen Lane   Mary Hacker
                          Rec. 1st July 1659.

p. 187. Willm Shirt of Lanc., planter, sells Wm Thatcher land on Fleet's
Bay, upon Haddaway's Creek, being 400 acres formerly taken by William
Shirt and Willm Lippiett. Dated 20th Dec. 1658.
Wit. Tho Medestard   signed Wm Shirt
      Sam Sloper (Hoker ?)
      Peter Knight   Rec. 1st July 1659.

p. 188. Power of Atty from Eppey Bonnison of the County of Lancaster to
"my loving friend Tobyas Horton" to ack. sale of land in Lanc. Co. called
Muskets Point. Dated 22nd March 1658/9.
Wit. Hugh Jordan   signed Ebby Bonnison
      Hugh Brent   Rec. 25th May 1659.

p. 189. Ebby Bonnison of Lanc., planter, sells Ever Peterson of same Co.,
planter, 350 acres on N. side of Rapa. River called Musket Point.
Dated 1st Feb. 1658/9.   signed Ebby Bonnison
Wit Hugh Brent
      Daniell Morleigh   Rec. 1st July 1659.

p. 189. Francis Benton of the County of Upper Norfolk, planter, in con-
sideration of L 400 sterl., pd by Lt. Coll. Anthony Elliott, sells 1250
acres of land in Rapa. River, "which land was granted to my Father John
Benton by patent dated October 13 1642 & descended unto me Francis Benton
as lawful heir of the sd John Benton and recovered from the Lady Elizabeth
Lunsford who was unlawfully possessed thereof by my Mother and guardian
Joane Reading by order of Court dated November 1st 1650."
Dated 4th October 1658.   signed Franc Benton
Wit. Roger Greene
      Tho Morrys   recognit 25 May 1659   rec 1 July 1659.

memo. That Livery & seizen was given by Francis Benton, etc., Dated 6th
October 1658.
Wit. Roger Greene
      Ch Hill
      Robt Varr
      John Rennolds
      Tho Obrizell   Recorded 1st July 1659.

Note: In the entries to follow a name appears as Godson and as Dodson.
I have simply followed the text, showing it as Edward Dale did. I believe
the name appears as Dodson in the Northumberland County records. B.F.

p. 190. Grant by Sam Matthews, Esq., to Mr. Gervayse Godson, 600 acres
in Lanc. Co., "on the south side of a creek opening out of Fleets bay
called Corotoman Creek", bounded S.E. upon land surveyed for Toby Horton,
"by some called Mr Wetherlyes land"; S.W. by land of John Taylor, decd.,
N.W. upon the main woods. This grant for the transpt. of 12 persons; names
not shown, into the colony.   signed Samuel Matthews
Dated 3rd March 1656/7.   W. Claybourne
                        Rec. 1 July 1659

p. 190. Gervayes Dodson sells for L40 sterling, to be paid in London by
Mr. Geo. Wale or his assigns to Coll. Will Clayborne, according to tenor
of three bills of Exchange, signed by Mr. Willm Strachey and directed to
Mr. Nicholas Trott at Vine Court in Bishops Gate Street, as also the value
of L 10 sterl. etc. Refers to the "said Gervayse Dodson of Northumberland
County." Dated 20th Dec. 1658.   signed Ger Dodson
Wit. Will Strachey
     Will Spicer
p. 191. Isbell wife of Gervays Dodson consents to above sale.
Wit. Gervayse Dodson   signed Isbell Dodson
                        recog 25 May 1659 rec 1st July 1659.

p. 191. Gervayes Dodson assigns to Mr. George Wale a survey of 500 acres
which joins a seat of 600 acres "due to me by patent & by me sold to the
sd Mr. George Wale lying in Lanc. Co. on the S. side of Corotoman Creek
near Wiccocomoco Indian Town which survey of 500 acres is entered with
rights in the office with Mr Tho Brereton." Dated 20th Dec. 1658.
Wit. Will Strachey   signed Ger Dodson
     Will Spicer

p. 191. Gervayse Dodson and wife Isbell appoint "our loving friend Thos
Jones" atty to ack sale of 600 acres to Mr. Geo. Wale, lying near the
Indian Town of Wiccocomoco, also 500 acres more, etc., Dated 24 May 1659.
Wit. Richd Nealmes   signed Ger Dodson
     Tho Shelton (sic)   Isbell Dodson
                        Recorded 25 May 1658 (sic)

p. 191. " Mr Thos Brereton   x x I have sold this land to Mr George Wale
& joining to it 500 acres assigned to me by Mr Thos Salisbury."
                        signed Ger Dodson
                        Recorded 1st July 1659.

p. 192. Regarding difference, referred to the Governor, betw Mr. John
Patte & Capt. Samuell Pensax, about 3 servants shipped on board the Nich
& Marg "whereof one is dead & two run away at Jamaica" Capt. Pensax to
deliver upon the arrival of the next ship from London, to John Patte, 2
sufficient men servants here in Virginia. Dated 7th June 1653.
                        signed Samuell Mathews
                        Rec. 1st Aug. 1659.

p. 192.　Joane Roughton (sic) "with the consent of my husband Willm Wroughton" (sic) gives Willm Abbey the younger a cow calf. 28 July 1659.
Wit.　Sam Gooch　　　　　　　　　signed Jone Wroughton
　　　　Eliz Robinson
　"Will Wroughton doth acknowledge this calfe in Court this 27th July 1659　WR　Test me Edwd Dale Cl Curt "
　　　　　　　　　　　　　　　Recorded 1st August 1659.

p. 193.　Jno Pine of Lanc., planter, sells 800 acres in Lanc. to Willm Neesham of Lanc. adj land occupied by Robt. Thompson. Dated 1st Dec. 1656.
Wit.　Edward Dale　　　　　　　　　signed　John Pine
　　　　Anth Stephens.
"Recognit in Curt 27 July 1659 - - John Pine & Annam uxorim ejus et record primo Augt sequent"

p. 193.　Willm Neesham of Lanc., planter, sells to Jno. Pine of Lanc., planter, 500 acres in Lanc. on N. side of Rapa.　Dated 5th Dec. 1656.
Wit.　Edward Dale　　　　　　　　　signed　Willm Neesham
　　　　Anthony Stephens
" recognit in Curt 27th July 1659 per dem Will Neesham et uxorem ejus et record primo Augt sequent per Edwd Dale Cl Cur"

p. 194.　John Sharpe of Lanc., planter, sells William Thompson of the same Co., planter, 300 acres on S. side Rapa., adj land late of Francis Browne now in possession of Nich Cooke.　Dated 23 July 1659.
Wit.　Dan Johnson　　　　　　　　signed　John Sharpe
　　　　Howell Powell　　　　　　　Rec. 1st Aug. 1659.

p. 195.　Grant from Sam Mathews, gent., etc. to Tho Powell 700 acres. 300 of this formerly granted Will Clapham, Jr., 15th Sept. 1657 and assigned by him to Thos. Powell, adj land of Anth Doney and the land of Capt. Thos Hackett and land formerly granted Thos. Powell 26th Feb. 1650.
Dated James City, 8th June 1658.　　signed　Sam Mathews
　　　　　　　　　　　　　　　　　　　　W Claybourne

p. 195.　Thos Powell & Howell Powell sell Will Clapham, senr., 700 acres.
Dated "last day of June 1659".　　signed　Tho Powell
Wit.　Walter Dickeson　　　　　　　　　How Powell
　　　　Richd Gorsuch　　　　　　Recorded 1st Aug. 1659

p. 195.　Edward Webb "with consent of Sara my wife" sells Henry Lane 220 acres described by patent dated 26th Feb. 1653, this land having been assigned to Webb by Thomas Bourne.　Dated 12 Jan 1658.
Wit. Geo Wadding　　　　　　signed Edward Webb
　　　　Tho Smith　　　　　　　　　　Sarah Webb
　　　　　　　　　　　　　Recorded 1st Aug. 1659.

p. 196. Henry Lane assigns foregoing to Richard Davyes. Dat.27 July 1659.
Wit. Howell Powell   signed Hen Lane
     Geo Waddinge   Rec. 1st Aug. 1659.

p. 196. Grant by Sam Mathews, etc., to George Thompson 4oo acres in
Lanc., bounded N. upon a creek called Tabs creek, Easterly upon Fleet's
Bay, South upon Nantopoizon Creek and West upon the main woods, distin-
guished by a line running So. from Tabs Creek to the main branch swamp
or run of Nank poizon Creek and thence to Bay. Dated James City 11th of
March 1657.   signed   Sam Mathews
                                  Rec. 1st Aug. 1659.

p. 196 "George Tomson with the consent of my wife Cleare Tomson" assigns
to Willm Angell 200 acres of above. Dated 26th July 1659.
Wit. Hugh Brent   signed George Thompson
     Hugh Jordan   Rec. 1st Aug. 1659

p. 197. Indenture made 26th July 1659, betw George Tompson & Willm
Angell of Lanc. Co., planter. Geo. Tompson "with the consent of my wife
Cleare Tompson" sells Wm Angell 200 acres, being half of a dividend of
400 acres in Lanc. Co., on so. side of a creek called Tabs Creek, which
issueth out of Fleets Bay.   signed Geo Thompson
Wit. Hugh Brent
     Hugh Jordan   Rec. 1st Aug 1659.

    Power of Atty from Geo Thompson to "my loving friend Hugh Brent"
to ack. right in land lying in Nantepoison Neck, 1/2 sold to Wm Angell
and the other half belonging to the "Relict of Thomas Howyak" (sic).
Dated 26th July 1659.   signed Geo Thompson
Wit Alexander Nash
     Hugh Jordan   Rec. 1st Aug. 1659.

p. 197. Enock Hawker sells cattle to Willm White, 10th Sept. 1659.
Wit.   Will Ball   signed Enock Hawker
        Sam Pensax   Rec. 1st Oct 1659.

p. 198. Will Ticknor gives bill to Mr Tho Griffith or Richard Gower or
either of them for 2000 lb "sweet scented tobacco in cask to be sorted
the one part of the plant the one way and the other way the sd tobacco
to be of my own crop x x to be paid 10 October next." Dat. 26 Dec. 1655.
Wit. Roger Radford   signed Will Tignor
      George Holmes   Rec. 1st 8ber 1659.

p. 198. John Robinson sells to Edward King 150 acres, being 1/2 of the
old patent of 300 acres where I did last live "at the back of Mr Foxes
Land where he now lives upon." Dated 28th Sept. 1659.
Wit. Jo Sharpe   signed Jo Robinson
     John Vause   Rec. 1st Oct.1659.

p. 199. Power of Atty from Peter Bonery and Marke Pensax of Stepney in the County of Middlesex, mariners, to "our loving friend Will Wroughton of Virginia in the County of Lancaster" to collect debts. Dated 31st July 1659.   signed   Peter Bonery
Wit.   Tho Roots   Marke Pensax
      Tho Marshall   Rec. 28th Sept. 1659.

p. 199. Joseph Maxes gives a heifer to Mary Malinge.
                    Rec. 1st October 1659.

p. 199. "Willm White and Anne my wife" sell Willm Thatcher 150 acres. Dated 25th Nov. 1657.   signed Willm White
Wit.   Tho Roots   Anne White
      Sam Gooch   Rec. 1st Oct 1659.

p.199. Power of Atty. "Anne White wife to Willm White of the County of Lancaster in Rappa" to "my loving Brother Willm Wraughton" to ack. sale of land to Will Thatcher. Dated 26th July 1659.
Wit.   Tho Roots   signed Anne White her mark
      Anne Hearne   Rec. 28th Sept. 1659.

p. 200. Grant Sam Mathews, etc., to Willm Shirt and Willm Lippitt 400 acres in Lanc. upon Fleet's Bay, beginning at the mouth of Haddaways Creek, running along the bay to a marked pine on the mouth of Corotoman Creek thence N.W. by W. up the sd creek to a marked "Porhickory" thence S.W. to a branch of Haddaways Creek and so down to the sd creek, thence down the sd creek where it first began. Dated James City, 1st Sept.1657.
                    signed   Samuell Mathews
                          W Claybourne
               Rec. 1st Sept 1659.

p. 200. Willm Lippitt assigns to Hugh Brent the above land and agrees to pay two cows and calves in case the land is "lost by order of Law and not through the sd Brents neglect in seating of it." Dated 8th May 1658.
Wit.   Tho Madestard   signed Will Lippiat
      Will Clappam   Rec. 1st October 1659.

p. 200. Indenture 10th July 1659. Betw Willm Lippeat and Hugh Brent of the County of Lanc., planter. Lippiat selling 1/2 of 400 acres in Lanc. Co., lying on the north side of a creek called Hadaway, etc.
Wit.   Tho Madestard   signed Will Lippiat
      Will Shirt   Rec. 1st Oct. 1659.

p. 2o1. Minor Minson and Robert Kempe sell to Roger Harrys 200 acres on S. side Rapa. betw the two head branches of Parretts Creek and adj land of Mr Francys Cole. Dated 19th March 1657/8. signed
Wit. The mark of David Precy (?)   Minor Minson
      David Rose his mark   Robert Kempe
                    Rec. 1st Oct. 1659.

60

p. 202. Grant from Edwd. Digges, etc., to Minored Minson and Robert Kempe, 200 acres at head of Parratts Creek. Dated James City 10 Dec 1656.
signed Edward Digges
W. Claybourne
Rec. 1st Oct. 1659.

p. 202. Roger Harrys and "Christian my wife" assign title to above to Thomas Warwicke. Dated 6th Nov. 1658.
Wit. Rich Perrott   signed Roger Harrys
     Minor Minson   Rec. 1st Oct. 1659.

p. 202. Power of Atty from Henry Portman of the parish of Putney in the County of Surrey, gent., to " my well beloved friend Mr Giles Webb of Chuckatuke, planter, in the plan'd of Virginia" to receive money that was "due and belonging to my Brother Mr Robert Portman decd who in his life time was a planter in the sd Island of Virginia". Dat. 8 Aug.1656.
Wit. Zorobabell Barker   signed Hen Portman
     John Ladyman

p. 203. Minor Minson and Robert Kempe assign right in patent (see p.202) 200 acres dated 10th Dec. 1656, to Roger Harrys. Dated 16th April 1658.
Wit. George Bradon   signed Robert Kempe
     his marke   Minor Minson
recognit in Curt 19 May 1657 Rec. 1 Oct.1657.

p. 203. " John Paine aged forty and four years or thereabouts sweareth that he did deliver by the order of Henry Corbyn to Mr John Holloway for the use of Capt John Whitey " (or Whitey ?) 1500 lbs. "of good porke in or about the month of December and further saith not."
Signed John Paine
"Taken before me Jo Curtys."   Recorded 13th Feb 1659/60.

p. 203.   Rappahannock Dec 26th 1659
Six day note of John Halloway, merchant, to Henry Corbyn promising to pay, in Barbados, 800 lb. "of the best sort of Muscovadoes sugar."
Wit. Zachariah Gillam   signed Jo Holwey
     Richard Cholmery   Recorded 13th Feb. 1659/60.

p. 204. Power of Atty. Moore Price to "my loving friend Thomas Maddeson" to ack land which "I and the said Thos Maddeson formerly bought of John Simpson." Dated 20th Nov. 1659.   signed Moore Price
Wit. Raleigh Travers   Rec. 30 Nov. 1659.

61

p. 204. Grant by Sam Mathews, etc., to Richard White, cooper, Evan Davys
and Sam Man of Rappa., 1000 acres in the Freshes of Rapa. River, adj.
land of Abraham Moone, near land of John Gillett and adj. land formerly
granted Richard White. Dated 6th Oct., 1658
                                    signed Sam Mathews
                                            W Claybourne
                        Rec. 30 Nov.1659.

p.204. Sam Man "with consent of my wife Margaret Man" assigns right in
above land to Richard White, cooper. Dated October 3rd 1659.
Wit. Jo Vause   signed Sam Man
      Mary Butcher   Margaret Man
                        Rec. 1 Dec. 1659.

p. 205. Power of Atty. Sam Man to Jno Vause to ack sale of above land
to Rich White, cooper, dated 3rd Sept 1659.
Wit. Fra Carpenter   signed Sam Man
      Mary Butcher   Margaret Man
                        Rec. 30th Nov. 1659.

p. 205. Howell Powell of Rapa. assigns to Charles Sneade "my full half
& part of land specified in this pattent." Dated 4th March 1652.
Wit. Jo. Payne   signed Howell Powell
                        Rec. 30th Nov. 1659.

p. 205. George Harrys of Rapa. assigns interest in land"specified in
this pattent " to Charles Snead. Dated 9 Dec. 1653.
Wit Howell Powell   signed Geo Harrys
                        Rec 30 Nov. 1659.

p. 205. Memorandum. Charles Sneade assigns interest in above land to Jno.
Paine of Rapa. Dated 21st Oct. 1654.
Wit. Hum Booth   signed Charles Sneade
                        Rec 1st Dec. 1659

p. 205. Memorandum. Charles Snead assigns interest in 400 acres to John
Paine of Rapa. Dated 21st Oct. 1654.
Wit. Hum Booth.   signed The mark of Charles Snead
                        Rec. 1st Dec. 1659.

p. 206. Elizabeth Sneade, the wife of the above sd. Charles Sneade gives
consent to assignment of her husband to Jno. Paine of above land.
Dated 15th April 1658.   signed Eliza Sneade
Wit. John Proper
      Francys Adkins   Rec. 1 Dec. 1659.

p. 206. George Harris assigns interest in land in above patent to Charles
Sneade. Dated 9th Dec. 1653.
Wit. Will Nesham
      Howell Powell   Rec. 1 Dec. 1659.

p. 206. Charles Sneade assigns interest in above land to Jo Paine of
Rappa. Dated 21st Oct. 1654.   signed Charles Sneade
Wit. Hum Booth
                        Rec. 1 Dec. 1659

p. 206. Memorandum. John Paine sells to Michaell Arme land in foregoing
transactions. Dated 5th Dec. 1659. signed John Paine
Wit. Edward Dale
        Jo Barrow   Rec. 1st March 1659/60.

p. 206. Memorandum. Margaret Paine, the wife of John Paine, gives consent
to sale of above land to Michaell Arme and appoints "my well beloved
friend Mr Edward Dale" atty. to ack. this in Court. Dated 19 Jan. 1659/60.
Wit. John Proper   signed Margaret Paine
        Jo Walker   Rec. 25th Jan 1659/60.

p. 207. "Mr Dale   I pray acknowledge ye in my behalfe the sale of 320
acres to Michaell Arme x x. " Dated 4th Jan. 1659/60.
Wit. John Walker   signed John Payne
        John Proper   Rec. 25th Jan. 1659.

p.207. Bill binding Tho Patteson to pay to Jo Brewer 800 lb. tobo.,
conveniently in Rappahannock River. Dated 7th Jan 1656/7.
Wit. James Bagnoll   signed Tho Pattison
        John Simpson
John Simpson by "letter of atty from Mr Jo Brewer assigns over all the
rights and title of this Bill unto Alex Porteus." Dated 3rd Feb 1656/7.
Wit. Bryan Stott (Scott ?)   signed Jo Simpson
                                     Rec. "primo Mareij 1659" (1659/60)

p. 207. Edwyn Connoway of Corotoman River sells to Will Gordon 200 acres.
This land adj. that of John Jones, was bought from John Meredith and for-
merly patented by Elyas Edmunds. Dated 30th March 1658.
Wit. John Hooper   signed Edwyn Connoway
        John Edwards   Rec. 1st Feb. 1660. (sic)

p. 208. "Whereas the Worshipfull the Commissioners of the County of
Lancaster In obedience to an order of assembly have by an order of Court
in their sd County appointed the Honbl Sr Wm Berkeley Governor & Capt
General of Virginia 8000 lb tobo due to him as by deverse orders of
assembly doth appear Now know Ye that I Peter Jennings being impowered by
the sd Honble Will Berkeley to receive the same as by a Letter under his
hand to Colo Cartor appears I do hereby authorize Mr Mathew Kempe to collect & receive tho same and his discharge upon the receipt thereof to be
full and effectuall to the discharge thereof witnes my hand this 6th day
of September 1660"   signed P Jennings
Wit. Rich Lee
        John Meredith   Rec 1 Febr 1660. (1660/1)

Note: Charles II had been proclaimed King on May 8th 1660. The population
of Virginia was estimated, at this time to be 30,000. B.F.

p. 208. Richard Davys of Lanc.,planter, appoints "my well beloved friend
John Needles"of the Co. of Lanc., planter, atty to collect debts,
Dated 18th March 1659/60.   signed Rich Davys
Wit. Edm Kemp
        Math Kempe   Rec. Mar. 14th 1660.

p. 209.   "I do authorize Mr Tho Chitwode to be a surveyor & do require
the Court of Lancaster to give him his oath given under my hand this 6th
of March 1660   signed   Will Berkeley
Jur in Curt 9th March 1660 Teste me Edw Dale Cl Curt"
                              Recorded 1st Apl. 1661.

p. 209.   "This Indenture made the 10th of January 1660 annoque Caroli
secundi XII x x John Meredith shipwright having sold 560 acres lying at
the head of Johns Creek joining land of Colo John Carter as by patent dated 10 October 1652 to George Marsh mercht and whereas the sd land was
again sold to Tho Carter decd which Thomas Carter in his Lifetime maslik-
ing the title of the sd George Marsh x x refused to pay the 8000 lb. of
tobo due x x This Indenture testifyeth that the sd George Marsh and his
wife for x x 7000 lb of tobo already paid have sold to Colo John Carter
the sd land and all the houses with all things belonging thereunto x x x
In witnes whereof the sd George Marsh and his wife Alice have hereunto
set their hand and seale the day and year above written"
Wit. David Milles   signed Geo Marsh
      Symon Kirbie   Alice Marsh
                              Recorded 1st Apl.1660.
Power of Atty. Alice Marsh to "my loving friend Mr Henry Corbyn" to ack.
consent. Dated 12th March 1660/1   signed Alice Marsh
Wit. Clemt Herbert
      Geo Price   Rec. 1st Apl. 1661.

p. 210. Mathew Kempe, gent., sells to Mr. Leonard Howson 2000 acres
commonly"called Turkey Cock hill in the County of Northumberland" for
400 pounds current English money. Dated 10th May 1661.
Wit. Robt Smyth   signed Matt Komp
      Davy Fox   Rec. 1 June 1661.

p. 210. Leonard Howson acks. debt to Mathew Kempe of 200 pounds and 4
men servants "and in the 13th year of the reign of our Sovereign Lord
King Charles the second". The conditions of the foregoing being L 100
to be paid in England on Dec. 1st next and to also pay on Dec. 1st next,
at Matthew Kempe's house 2 men servants "not exceeding the age of thirty"
with "such beding and clothing as they bring with them x x".
Wit. Robt Smith   signed Leon Howson
      Davy Fox   Rec. 1st June 1661.

p. 211. Further agreements of Leonard Howson to pay Matthew Kempe.

Note: According to this, it seems as though Mr. Oliver Cromwell and some
others were mistaken. Perhaps Col. Carter or Sir William Berkeley could
have informed us. B.F.

p. 211. Power of Atty. Philip Mallory of Virginia, in the County of York,
Clerk, to Mr. Mathew Kempe of the County of Lancaster, gent., to make de-
livery of a parcel of land "of a thousand acres sictuate in the aforesd
County of Lancaster in Fleets Bay (formerly belonging unto Humphrey Tabb
decd) as by pattent appearing unto Robert Bristow and Edmond Welsh jointly
by stick & turfe according to the Laws & customes of England x x"
Dated April 8th 1661.   signed Philip Malory
Wit. Roger Malory   Recorded 8th May 1661.

p. 212. John Simpson sells to Ennys Mcconathey and Robert Rosse a parcel of land being part of a patent of 600 acres bought by Simpson from Alex Porteus. Dated 4th May 1661.   signed Jo Simpson
Wit. Will Stookes
      Bryan Stott (Scott ?)   Rec. 1 June 1661.

p. 212. Power of Atty. John Dannell, mariner, belonging to the ship Amity, Samuell Pensax Commander, to "my loving friend Will Neesham x x to demand of Thomas Chetwode one able man servt well in health which sd servt is to be paid at the arrivall of the first ship the year following the date here-of." Dated 24th March 1661.   signed John Dannell
Wit. Jo Pine
      Robt Osborne   Rec. 8th May 1661.

p. 212. Power of Atty. Edmond Faroe of the City of London, mariner, to Will Neesham of Rapa. River in Virginia, gent., to receive from Hugh Hinsoy (Rinsey ?) of Rappa., planter, and others debts "due me or to one John Fish Citizen & fletcher of London." Dated 15 March 1660/1.
Wit. John Pine   signed Edmond Faroe
      Will Hawkes
      John Merryman   Rec. 8th May 1661.

p. 213. George Kibble relinquishes interest in bill of sale. Dated 20th July 1659.   signed Geo Keble
Wit John Humphreyes
      James Bonner   Rec. 8th May 1661.

p. 213. Will Dudley of Pianketank assigns right in bill to Tho Hill also of Pianketank. Dated 11th March 1660/1. signed Will Dudley
Wit. Thomas - inye (the first letter of the last name omitted here
               appears as though it might be an A or a Q.)
Wit. Christopher Shepherd
    "Satisfaction being made by me Thomas Hill on due and lawful con-sideration as witnes my hand 8 Maij anno 1662" (sic)
                      signed Will Dudley
               Rec. 1 June 1662.
    "Mr Dale
        My love remembered Sir I shall desire you to acknowledge a bill of sale in Court of Land to the bearer hereof Thomas Hill and this my note shall impower you as fully as if I myselfe were there present not more at present but rest   Your lo friend
May 7th 1660   Will Dudley "
               Rec. 8th May 1661.

p. 214. "Received April 29th 1661 of John Meredith 800 lb tobo for the amount of Mr Peter Knight of Wicoocomoco in part of a Judgmt of 2000 lb. tobo I say these received   Hen Corbyn "
Recorded 1 June 1661.

p. 214. Grant from Edwd. Digges, etc., to Thomas Roots, 50 acres in Lanc. adj. a seat of 80 acres granted Edward Grymes, decd., and adj. two other seats granted Grymes. Dated 15th June 1655.
Rec. 8th May 1661.

John Edwards, Chirurgeon, and Executor to the Estate of Mr. Tho. Roots, decd., assigns title to above to Will Wroughton. Dat. 11 Apl.1661.
Wit. Will Ball   signed John Edwards
    James Bidlccom   Rec. 1 June 1661.

p. 214. "Bryan Stott and Thomas Stott being two brothers" purchased from Alexander Portous 600 acres. This land formerly belonged to Lambert Lambothson and Richard Hatton and now in possession of the Stotts. They devide the land betw. themselves. Dated 27th April 1661.
Wit. John Simpson   signed Bryan Stott
    Giles Cowch   Tho Stott
Recorded 1st June 1661.
Note: The above name may be Stott or Scott. B.F.

p. 215. Tho Stott gives to "Eliz Stott the daughter of Bryan Stott one year old heifer" Dated May 6th 1661.   signed Tho Stott
Wit. Jno Simpson   Recorded 1st June 1661.

Note: This name appears to be Scott to me but I am informed that I am mistaken-that the name is Stott. B.F.

p. 215. David Fox sells to Benjamyn Powell 100 acres about 2 miles from "where the sd Fox liveth" Dated 14th Sept 1651. (sic)
Wit. John Sharpe   signed Davi Fox
    Thomas Thrashar   Recorded 8th May 1661.

Note: Not the first Ben who appears to have been jammed in. B.F.

p. 215. Thos Coggin assigns right to bill to Will Clappam, Senr.
Dated - September 1657.   No signature shown on record.
Wit. John Macksurson
    Nich Garner   Recorded 8th May 1661.

Thos Coggin assigns right to bill to Will Denbigh. Dated 4th November 165-.   signed Tho Coggin
No witnesses shown on record.   Recorded 8th May 1661.

p. 216. Power of Atty. Thomas Coggan, seaman, to "my loving friend Will Clappam, Senior" to collect debts from David Fox. Dated 15th Apl. 1661.
Wit. Will Hutchinson signed Tho Coggan
      Edward Lunsford   Rec. 8th May 1661.

p. 216. Sam Mathews, etc., to Mr Grey Skipwith, 900 acres in New Kent County on the N. side of Mattopony River "runing down the river south to the marked tree of Mr Digges his land x x". Given at James City 11th October 1658.

p. 216. "Sr Gray Skipwith Barronett" for "natural love and affection I bear unto Eliz Kempe my Daughter in Law" gives the above land to her.
Dated 10th July 1661. signed Gray Skipwith
Wit. Matt Kempe
      Cuth Potter   Recorded 10th July 1661.

p. 217. Mr. Thos Bries of Lanc., by agreement dated 20th Jan. 1656, sold to John Edwards of the sd Co., Chirurgeon, a tract of land known as "popolar neck." x x "In case of the mortality of the sd Thos Bries" he gave power to Edward Dale of the same Co., gent., upon payment, to make conveyances. Payment being made Dale conveys the land. Dated 10th July 1661. signed Edward Dale
Wit. Cuth Potter
      Edward Roe   Recorded 1st Aug. 1661.

p. 217. Jane Clarke of the Co. of Lanc.,relict of Arthur Clarke, lately decd., gives "to my son Will Clarke" various cattle when he comes of age. "x x should he die before he attains the age of 17 the afsd cattle to return to myself or next heir." Dated 27th Nov. 1660.
Wit. Tho Daniell signed Jane Clarke
      Tho Naylor
             Jane Clarke appoints Mr John Sharpe and Mr Will Neesham as overseers of the above gift for the use of Willm Clarke. No date shown.
Wit. Will Hall signed Jane Clarke
      Tho Daniell
             "I Will Linnell (sic) do here acknowledge to this deed of gift and do hereunto set my hand and seale"
                     In place of signature there is simply "the seale".
                     Recorded 1st August 1661.

p. 218. Jenkyn Price did stand indebted to Ever Peterson 2001 lb of tobo, for which he bound over a servt, etc. Having failed in payment and Peterson being willing to stand until next crop, Price mortgages all his Estate agreeing to pay 30th Nov. next. Date 11th May 1661.
Wit. John Carter signed Jenkyn Price
      Symon Kirby   Rec. 1st Aug 1661.

p. 219. Agreement regarding land betw Thos Steede and Jno Cosens. Refers to Sarah Steede now wife of Thos Steede. Dated 23rd Feb. 1660/1.
Wit. Hugh Brent   signed Tho Steede
     Tho Hobson   John Cosens
                       Rec. 1st Aug. 1661.

p. 219. Grant by Sam Mathews to John Jones 350 acres on Corotoman River. Dated 22nd March 1657/7.   signed Sam Mathews
                          W Claybourne Sec

p 220. John Jones binds himself to forfeit L 100. if unable to make good title to above land to Thos Chetwode and Thos Perryn. Dated 15 Sept 1659.
Wit. Wm Bawdes (?)   signed John Jones
     Will Allison   Rec. 1st Aug.1661.

p. 220 Power of Atty. John Jones to Mr Peter Knight to ack sale of above land. Dated 25th Feb. 1659/60.   signed John Jones
Wit. James Hawley
     Edward Hawley   Rec. 10th July 1661.

p. 220. Power of Atty. Will Lorkyn, boatwright, to Edward Roe of Lanc. Dated 23rd Jan 1660/1.   signed Wm Lorkyn
Wit. Leonard Cacott   Rec. 10th July 1661.

p. 220. Sir Wm Berkeley, Governor of Virginia, by commission from the King, dated 30th July 1660, given permission to leave the colony. Col. Fran Morrison to be Governor and Captain Gen'l. of Virginia. His authority to begin upon the Governors setting sail.
        signed: Will Berkeley   Edw Hill
              Tho Ludwell Sec   Hen Browne
              Tho Pettus   and
              Hen Perry   Tho Swanne

"Vera Copia Test Tho Brereton Copia Concordat Test Hen Randolph Cl Dom Com
Mr Corbyn   Please send a copy of this to your other County & to the Countys of Potomack attested by your Clerk   Yours
                                  Hen Randolph
record in Curt 10 die Julij anno 1662 por Edw Dale Cl Cur "

p. 221. "Surveyed the 24th of June 1661 for Will Clapham Junr son to Will Clapham decd" 200 acres lying in Fleet's Bay, being part of 600 acres belonging to Tobias Horton upon the N. side of Hadaways Creek.
                  signed Tho Chetwode
                Recorded 10th July 1661.

p. 221. John Edwards, Chirurgeon in the Co. of Lancr., gives to Will White, jun., son to Will White, senr., in afsd Co., "one pied heifer being Mr Tho Roots his mark x x x if sd Will White Jun die without heir of his body then the heifer to the next of his fathers children x x" Dated 20th March 1660/1.   signed John Edwards
Wit. James Biddlecombe
      Dm Theryott   Rec. 1st Aug. 1661.

p. 222. Indenture made 17th Sept 1661 betw. Uriah Angell and Willm Garrett of the Co. of Lanc. confirming to Garrett half of a tract of land of 400 acres on S. side of a creek called Tabbs Creek which issueth out of Fleet's Bay.   signed Uriah Angell
Wit. Hugh Brent   Recog. 13th Nov. 1661.
      John Cono.   Recorded 1 Jan 1661/2.

p. 222. Indenture made 29th Oct. 1661. Wm Garrett sells to Magne Barrett of Lanc, 100 acres, part of above, with his wife's consent. Wife's name not shown.   signed Will Garrett his mark
Wit. Will Canille
      Roger Kelly   Recorded 1st Jan 1661/2.

p. 223. Indenture dated 13th Nov. 1661. Thomas Chetwode of Co. of Lanc., merchant, sells to Willm Travers of the same Co., merchant, 500 acres on the branches of Morattico, adj. land of Charles Grymes, clerk.
Wit. Alex Fleming   signed Thos Chetwode
      Math Kempe   Rec. 1st Jan 1661/2.

p. 223. Robert Middleton of Co. of Lanc., planter, sells to Thos. Kid of the same co., planter, 250 acres "at the head of Mr Burnhams Creek" adj. land of "sd Middleton and Willys", land of Thos Pattison and Robt Chowning the sd land due on a patent to Middleton dated 16th Jan 1658/9.
Dated 27th Dec. 1660.   signed Robt Middleton
Wit. Robt Chowninge
      Tho Pattison
      Tho Widowes
      Johen Stevenson   Recorded 1st Jan 1661/2.

p. 224. Power of Atty. Robt. Middleton and Mary his wife to Mr. Henry Corbyn to ack. bill of sale of Dec 26th 1660 on 260 (sic) acres. Dated 26th Dec. 1660.   signed Robt Middleton
Wit. Nich Archer   Mary Middleton
      John Harris   Recorded 13th - - 1661.

p. 224. Wm Wroughton of Corotoman in Co. of Lanc., having formerly leased
to Nicholas Hale and Robert Pollard, land, etc., extends lease ten years
from New Years day next. This is a long and complicated legal instrument.
Dated 18th July 1661.   signed Will Wroughton
Wit. Hen Ward   Nich Hale
      Will Thomas   Robt Pollard
William Wroughton acks receipt of two servants according to above lease.
Dated 10th Oct. 1661.   signed Will Wroughton
Wit. John Fletcher
      Tho Daniel   Recorded 1st Jan 1661/2.

p. 226. Henry Danson of Standley (or Handley) hundred upon Warwicke river
in the County of Warwicke in Virginia, being attorney of Mr. Robert Dixon
the true and lawful brother of Mr Miles Dixon, late of Rapa., decd., sells
to Edward Roe of Machapungo in Lancaster County, all the plantation known
as Machapungo, lying betw plantations of Colo. Robt. Smyth and Colo
Anthony Ellyotts. Also other land. Dated 12th Nov.1661.
Wit. Raw Travers   signed Hen Dawson atty of
     Cuth Potter   Mr Robt Dixon
     Will Leech   Rec. 1st Jan 1661/2.

p. 227. Agreement 1st Nov 166- betw Dnc Therriott of the Co. of Lanc.,
planter,   and   John Fletcher and Joseph Bayley of the same Co. planters. Lease of plantation whereon Peter Godson lately lived, 1600 acres,
for 14 years from Dec. 25th next.   signed Dm Therriott
Wit. Hen Corbyn
      Abra Weekes   Recorded 1st January 1661/2

p. 229. John Fish Citizen and fletcher of London, gives power of atty
to Edmond Farow of London, mariner, to collect debts from Hugh Kinsey of
Rapa. in Virginia, planter, and from others. Dated 18th Sept. 1660.
Wit. Rich Donley   signed John Fish
      John Fisher
      John Neenee
      Will Bayley
      Anth Cheeke   Recorded 12th March 1661/2.

p. 229. Grant by Sam Mathews to John Nichols of Corotoman, 900 acres on
S. side of Corotoman river. Bounded on E. by land of Mr. Edwyn Connoway,
on S.W. by land of Nich George and Andrew Bowyer, on S.W. also by land
of Geo. Goldsmith, on S.E by lands of Mr. Kinsey and Elyas Edmonds,decd.
etc. Dated 18th March 1657/8.   signed Sam Mathews
                                               W Claybourne Sec
                         Recorded 14th May 1662.

p. 230. John Nichols sells above 900 acres to John Edwards of Lanc. Co.,
cooper. Dated 11 Jan 1661/2.   signed John Nichols
Wit. George Flower
      Mary Flower   Recorded 1st June 1662.

p. 231. Joane Davyes of the parish of St Leonards Shoreditch, in the
County of Midd., widow, Executrix of Richard Davyes of Peanketanck river
in Virginia, "my late husband decd" gives power of attorney to "my trusty
and well beloved friend John Brereton of Poanketanck river in Virginia
planter", to receive of Mr. John Needles of Peanketanck river, planter,
admr of the estate of "my late husband Rich Davyes of Peanketanck river
planter decd", debts from various persons. Dated 3rd July 1661.
Wit. Sam Pensax   signed Joane Davyes
      Geo Seaton
      Edw Tudman (?)   Recorded 14th May 1662.

p. 232. Grant from Sam Mathews, etc., to Lambert Moore and Bartholomew
Linton 412 acres on N. side of Piankotank river. Dated 17th Feb. 1658/9.
                                    signed Sam Mathews
                                            W Claybourne Sec
                        Rec. 14th May 1662.
      Lambert Moore assigns his interest in above to Bartholomew Linton.
Dated 14th December 1660.   signed Lambert Moore
Wit. Robert Osborne   Eliz Moore
      John Davyes   Rec. 14th May 1662.

      Bartholomew Linton sells to Robt Smyth of Lanc. Co., above land.
Dated 11th December 1661.   signed Bartholomew Linton
Wit. Tho Wroth
      Richard Kintish   Rec. 14th May 1662.

p. 233. Power of Atty. Bartholomew Linton to Thos. Chetwode to ack. sale
of above land to Collo. Robert Smyth. Dated 20th Jan.1661/2.
Wit. D Therriott   signed Bartholomew Linton
      Edward Dale   Rec. 14th May 1662.

p. 233. Francys Weekes of the County of Lanc.,widow, for love and
affection "I bear to Anne Barlow my Daughter" gives "all my whole Estate
whatsoever x x as well in England as in Virginia." Dated 13th May 1662.
Wit. Leonard Howson   signed Fran Weekes
     Cuth Potter   Rec. 14th May 1662.

p. 233. Grant from Francys Moryson to Colo. John Carter 450 acres, adj.
land of Thomas Chetwode, etc. Dated 25th Sept. 1661.
                                    signed Francis Moryson
                                            Tho Ludwell Sec
                        Rec. 14th May 1662.

p. 234. Col. John Carter assigns above land to Thomas Marshall. Dated 14th
May 1662.   signed John Carter
No witnesses shown.   Rec. 14th May 1662.

      Thomas Marshall assigns half of above, 225 acres adj. land of
Thos Chetwode to Will Cooke and John Potter. Dated 14th May 1662 .
                                    signed Tho Marshall
                        Rec. 14th May 1662.

p. 234. Thos Marshall assigns upper part of foregoing land, 225 acres to Wm Hutchins.　　　　　　　　　signed Tho Marshall
　　　　　　　　　　　　　Rec. 14th May 1662
p. 234. William Hutchins assigns above 225 acres to Edward King and Samuell Gooch. Dated 14th May 1662.　　signed Will Hutchins
No witnesses shown.　　　　　　Recorded 14th May 1662

p. 235.　"Anne Johnson widow and relict to Daniel Johnson lately decd and Exr to Randolph Chamblett do for my heirs Exrs and assignes assign over all my right title" to 100 acres of land to Mr. John Haslewood.
Dated 13th March 1661/2.　　　　　signed Ann Johnson
Wit. John Edwards
　　　Leonard Cacott.　　　　　Rec. 14th May 1662.

p. 235.　Thos Chetwode of Lanc. gent., sells to William Wroughton of sd. County, 350 acres lying on Eastermost branch of Corotoman River which formerly was patented in Mr. Jones name, that married Mrs. Moone's Daughter, and since taken up in sd. Thos. Chetwode's name. Dat.1 Mar 1661/2
Wit.　D Therriott　　　　　　signed Thos Chetwode
　　　Tho Danniell　　Recog 12 Mar 1661　rec 1 Apl 1661 (sic)

p. 235.　Bristoll. Indenture made 21st June 1661. Thos Gaynor agrees to serve George Hancocke, from date hereof until his first next arrival at Virginia, and after for four years.　"In consideration whereof the sd master doth hereby covenant and grant to and with the sd servant to pay for his passing and to find and allow him meat drink apparroll Lodging with other necessarys during the sd terme and at the end of the sd terme to pay unto him one ax one hoe one years provision double apparell fifty acres of land according to the Custome of the Country"
"Inrolled upon record　　　　　signed　Tho Gaynor
according to the custome
of the sd City　the City seale"
Witness　And Hayes　　　　Recorded 1st April 1662.

　　　　　　　　　　　　　(sic)
p. 236.　Grant from Francis Morryson to Thomas Graves, Senr., 700 acres on branch of Corotoman river. Dated 20th March 1661/2.
　　　　　　　　signature　not shown on record.
　　　　　　　　Rec. 14th May 1662.

p. 236. Thomas Grymes, senr. (This evidently entered upon the record in error since the name appears as Graves in the grant above and also twice in the entry to follow as Graves.) of Timber Neck Creek in the County of Gloucester, planter, sells to Mr. John Edwards of Lancaster, Chirurgeon, 700 acres above. Dated 14th May 1662.
Wit. Anth Stephens　　　　　signed　Tho Graves Senr　(sic)
　　　Edward Sanders　　　　Recorded 1st June 1662.

72

p. 237. 21st May 1662. Hugh Kinsey of Lanc., planter, mortgages to John Fish of London, Fletcher, plantation "whereon the sd Hugh Kinsey now liveth", 500 acres, for 33 pounds six shillings to be paid 20th Jan.next.
Wit. Miles Riley   signed Hugh Kinsey
     Edward Dale   recognit 9 July 1662 rec 1 Aug. 1662.

p. 238. William Wroughton sells to Robert Swann 175 acres. 21st May 1662.
Wit. Edmond Lewys   signed Will Wroughton
     Tho Danniell   Rec. 1st Aug 1662.

p. 239. Thomas Williams of Morattrie in County of Lanc., planter, sells to John Chynn of same Co., planter, and Henry Davys of the same, shipwright, land originally granted by Sir William Berkeley to Davyd Fox, gent.
Dated 3rd July 1662.   signed Tho Willyams
Wit. Raw Travers
      Edward Dale   Rec. 1st Aug. 1662.

p. 240. Thos Willyams sells cattle to Chynn and Davys. Dated 3 July 1662.
Wit. Rawleigh Travers   signed Tho Willyums
     Edward Dale   Rec 1st Aug 1662.

p. 241. " Know all men by these presents that I Davyd Fox of the County of Lancr in Rappahannock river in Virga gent as wel for the natural love & affection wch I bear unto Hannah ffox my daughter as also for divers other good causes x x x give grant alein bargain sel enfeoff & confirm unto Robt Tomlyn of the County of Rappa in Rappahannock River aforsd planter all those lands plate negroes cattle household stuff goods and chattels whatsoever x x x vizt all that my plantation containing 800 acres x x lying x x in the x x County of Rappah near the mouth of Piscaticoon creek x x now in the occupation of me the aforesd Davyd Fox x x and also all my plate I am now possessed with all Vizt three dozen of large silver spoones marked D:F:M: one large sullibub dish with a cover   one large tanckerd containing one pestle one large caudle cup engraven about one quart   one sugar box in form of a scollup shel ene engraven fruit dish with a foot one large salt celler two smaller and one trencher salt two large substantial porrenger marked D:F:M: one wyne bowle one large sack cup   one large dram cup one large bason containing about one gallon one plain caudle cup wth three legs one plain fruit dish   one silver drinking bowle one old silver spoone   six negroes vizt Wingo x x x x " Dated 11th November 1662. signed Davy ffox
Wit. Edward Dale
     John Dawe   Recorded 12 Nov.1662 Edward Dale Cl Cur

Note: As usual no punctuation here. I've endeavored to space the words in the abstract to indicate each item-thereby depriving the reader of that pleasure. Whereas I would be overjoyed to own any of these, either the "sugar box" or the large bason containing about one gallon would be my choice sight unseen. It prob. took all six negroes to keep this silver clean. No forks. This makes us a bit uncomfortable when one comes to consider Mrs. Fox's costumes to be listed later. B.F.

p. 242. Robert Chowning agrees that a line of trees marked at the date of this, in the presence of Mr. Jo Vause and James Lidsey, to be "a ful and authentic"division of 580 acres patented 4th April 1658 by Thomas Patteson and himself. Dated 23rd Dec. 1659.
Wit. Jo Vause   signed Robt Chowning
     James Lidsey
Memo. Thos Patteson sells his part of above land to Hen Nichols. Dated the "last of April 1662".   signed Tho Patteson
Wit. Robt Chowning

Power of Atty. Tho Patteson to his "lo friend Hen Nicholas" to ack div. of land. Dated 7th June 1662.   signed Tho Patteson
No witnesses shown on record.

Tho Patteson agrees to above, dated as above. signed Tho Patteson.
Wit. John Vause
      Thos Lidsey   Recorded 1st Nov. 1662.

p. 243. Tho Pattison "of the County of Rappati" sells to Hen Nicholas of Lanc., planter, 400 acres being part of land granted to Robt. Chowning and himself, as above. Dated "last day of April 1662"
Wit. Robt Chowning.   signed Tho Patteson
                                       Anne Patteson
                       Recorded 1st Nov. 1662.

Memo. Anne Patteson, the wife of Tho Patteson, consents to above sale and appoints "my lo friend Dmi Theriot" to ack. this in Court. Dated "last of April 1662"   signed Anne Patteson
Wit. Tho Maddeson
     Anth Richardson   Recorded 10th Sept.1662.

p. 244. Power of Atty. Tho Patteson and Anne Patteson to Mr Richd Perrot to ack sale of land to Hen Nicholas. Dated 17th June 1662.
Wit. Edward Hall   signed Tho Patteson
     Jone Hodger her mark   Anne Patteson
                       Recorded 10th Sept 1662.

Note: We hope, after all this, that Henry Nichols or Nicholas had peace and prosperity upon his land. B.F.

p. 244. James Botler of Nansimond "in right of my wife Mary daughter to Michael Wilcocks" assigns claim to 300 acres patented by Wm Dura- - (illegible) upon Rappate River to Peter Montague. Dated 2nd June 1662.
Wit. Richd Smith   signed Ja Botler
     Will Drinkwater   Mary Botler
                       Recorded 10th Sept 1662.

Power of Atty. James Botler and Mary Botler to Nicholas Cooke, atty, to ack. above sale.   signed James Botler
Wit. Richd Smith   Mary Botler
     Will Drinkwater   Recorded 10th Sept 1662.

74

p. 245   Ebbya Bonnison sells to Hugh Brent and Tobias Horton of Lanc.,
planters, 200 acres on N. side of Haddaway Creek and on the S. side of
Corotoman Creek, which was the land that was divided betw. Hugh Brent
and Ebbya Bonnison, as "by pattent will more large appear". Dat.8 Sept.
1662.   signed Abya Bonnison
Wit. John Wortham
      John Lidsig (Lidsey ?)   Rec. 1st Nov. 1662.

Power of Atty. Hannor Bonnison to John Cone (Cane ? Cane ?) to ack sale
of above land by her husband Ebbya Bonnison. Dated 8th Sept 1662.
Wit. John Wortham   signed Honnor Bonnison
      John - - -   Rec. 1st Nov. 1662.

p. 246. Teage Correll binds himself to pay Tobias Horton 8000 lb tobo.
Payments to be made yearly of 1500 lb. per year beginning 10th Oct.next.
Dated 6th Nov.1662.   signed Teage Carroll
Wit. Hugh Brent
     Uriah Angell   Rec. 1st Nov.1662.
Tobyas Horton sells to Teage Corrall of Lanc., planter, 100 acres, lying
betw. two creeks that issueth out of ffleets bay called by name Tabbs
Creek and Penteyson (Antipoison ?) Creek. Dated Nov.6th 1662.
Wit. Hugh Brent   signed Tobyas Horton
      Uriah Angell   Rec. 12th Nov. 1662.
p. 247. Power of Atty. Eliz Horton to "my loving son in Law Uriah Angell"
to ack above sale. Dated 6th Nov.1662. signed Eliz Horton.
Wit. Hugh Brent
      John Trotman   Rec. 12th Nov.1662.

Note: These records seem to indicate that the Lancaster County name
Currell may have originally been Carroll. It also appears as Correll.B.F.

p. 247. Aug. 21st 1662. John Simons agrees to serve Samuell Tilghman from
"the date hereof until his first or next arrival in Virginia or Maryland"
and during the next four years.   signed Sam Tilghman
Wit. Wm - - -
     Edward Peires   Rec. 12th Nov. 1662.

p. 248. Richard Lewys of Lanc., planter sells to Thomas Tuskwell (?) in
Co., afsd. 100 acres adj. land of Mr. Cuthbert Potter and land of Mr. Tho.
Willys. Dated 20th August 1662.   signed   Richd Lewys
Wit. Will Pew   ffran Lewys
      Will Perry   Rec. 1st Dec. 1662.

p. 250. Will Clapham of Lanc., planter, sells John Berry of Lanc., planter
350 acres, being part of a patent granted Tho Powell 8th June 1658. This
land formerly held by Howell Powell and assigned to Clapham by Tho and
Howell Powell. Dated 25th August 1652. signed Will Clapham
Wit. Tho Brereton   Jane Clapham
      Edward Lunsford   Recorded 1st Dec. 1662.

p. 249. John Curtys of Lanc., gent., sells to Davyd Allyson of Lanc., planter, "all that plantation whereon the sd Davyd Allyson now liveth", 260 acres adj. land of Abraham Moone. Dated 6th Nov. 1662.
Memo. "Anne Curtys the wife of the above named John Curtys" agrees to sale.
Wit. Willm Howeman   signed John Curtys
  Robt. Prise   Anne Curtys
         Recorded Dec. 1st 1662.

p. 250. Richard Merriman of Lanc.,planter, binds himself to deliver to Davyd ffox of Lanc., gent., "too men servants", Will Cook and Samuel Howard and one maid servt, Rebecca Pattin, and also cattle, for thirty pounds sterling payable 24th Jan 1662 in London. Dated Jan 24th 1662/3.
Wit. Robt Goodyeare   signed Richd Merriman
  Will Stephens   Rec. 1st Feb. 1662/3

p. 251. Edw. Roe of Lanc., planter, sells to Robt. Smith of Lanc.,gentle-man, 50 acres now occupied by Roe. Pmt to be forty pounds current English money by bills of Exchange, payable 1st of May next. Dated Jan - 1662/3.
Wit. John Curtys   signed Edw Roe
  Cuthbert Potter   Rec. 1st Feb. 1662/3.
Power of Atty. Mary Roe wife of Edward Roe to Cuthbert Potter to ack. sale of above land. Dated 24th Jan 1662/3.
Wit. Christopher Withnell   signed Mary Roe
  Robt. Carnehill   Recorded 28th Jan 1662/3.

p. 252. Benjamin Whiscombe of London, Marriner, sells to John Rayney of Lanc., planter, 221 acres "all the plantation the sd John Rayney now liveth on." Dated 26th Jan 1662/3. signed Ben Whiscom
Wit Edward Dale
  Eliz Turner   Recorded 1st Feb 1662/3

p. 253. Benjamin Whiscom of London, Marriner, sells to John Rayney cer-tain cattle and hogs, "late purchased by me the afsd Benjamin Whiscom and one Jos Allen dec of Alexander Porteus late likewise decd. Dat.26 Jan 1662.
Wit. Edward Dale   signed Ben Whiscom
  Eliz Turner   Rec 1st Feb. 1662/3.

p. 253. Jane Clapham ack. that her husband has sold to John Berry a tract of land on Corotoman River commonly called Honey Point. Dated 10th December 1662.   signed Jane Clappam
Wit. Thomas Coggan
  John Hallett   Recorded 1st Feb.1662.

p. 254. Power of Atty. Jane Clappam wife to Will Clappam to John Nichols
Dated 21st January 1662/3.   signed Jane Clappam
Wit. Will Smith   "Recognit in cur 28 Jan ano 1662 " (1662/3)

p. 254. Power of Atty. Will Thatcher of Corotoman, in Lanc., to Will Hutchins. Does not state what for. Dated 21st Jan 1662/3.
Wit. Henry Shepheard   signed Will Thatcher
      Tho Reynolds
      Geo Hanson   Recorded 28th Jan. 1662/3.

Note; Before reading the following the writer would like to ask one question of the reader. Have you ever even walked through a tobacco field in Tidewater Virginia on a hot June mid-day ? Living far to the north for many years, I somehow understand why Marsh, Jones, Dikes, Phillips and Benson went on that summer's jaunt. Whereas this record does not and cannot state all, Henry Corbin certainly is to be commended, considering his day and generation, for his moderation in this instance. A Virginia man and a gentleman he knew exactly why they went. B.F.

p. 254. "These may certify that Mr Henry Corbin did bring before me Evan Jones who did swear to me that he and four more did about the 28th of June runaway wth his masters boat and did not return to his sd master til the 16th day of Decemb and that he had no cause given him for his so doing and also Geo Dikes did confess he did as the sd Jones at the said time runaway and also Will Phillips and that neither of them had any cause given them and that they did return to their sd master upon the 19th day of Septemb and said that Tho Marsh was the chief cause of their going
                              signed Richd Perrott "
                    Recorded 11th March 1662/3.

p. 255. "Whereas Mr Henry Corbyn brought before me two of his servts the one named Tho Marsh who confessed himself to have runaway wth others the 20th of June last and returned to his masters house again the first of August following the other named Edmd Benson who runaway in the company of the afsd Marsh the 20th of June last with their masters boat and returned not til the 19th of September following and that they had no cause given them by their mastr or any other for their running away this at my house this 8th Decemb: 1662.   signed George Marsh "
                    Recorded 11th March 1662/3

p. 255. William Rowze of Corotoman, planter sells cattle to Tho Hopkins of the Dividing Creek, planter. Dated 10th March 1662/3.
Wit. Marke Pensax   signed Will Rowze
      Robt. Farrington   Rec. 1st April 1663.

p. 255. "Whereas at a County Court held at the Isle of Wight the 9th of Octob: 1648 It was ordered that Will Clapham should deliver and resign unto Capt George ffawdon all the estate of Will Wright mercht and his right of administration upon the sd estate and thereupon"-Clapham is released from bond, etc. "Given under my hand and the signet of the Council this 20th of July 1651"   signed Robert Huberd
                                        Cl record
                    Recorded in Lanc. 11th March 1662/3.

p. 256. Berhum Obert of Lancaster Co., by the last will and Testament of his father, Barkum Obert late of the same County, decd., had 200 acres bequeathed to him. "Whereas the sd Barham Obert decd was an alien and no free borne subject" the land was escheated. Upon application to the Governor (Morrison) on "27 of 7th last past" this land was granted to Hobert. He now sells it to John Vause. Dated 3rd December 1662.
Wit. Cuth Potter   signed Barhum Obert
      Will Brett   Recorded 1st April 1663.

p. 256. "Mr Merideth   I desire you for to pay unto Hen Herde for my use the sum of four hundred pounds of tobacco and taking his receipt x x
Jan 10 1661   Your lo Friend
                                              Peter Knight "
                                  Recorded 11th March 1662/3.

p. 257. Grant from Frances Moryson, etc., to John Ashley 240 acres. Dated 16th June 1662.
        John Ashley assigns above to Tho Chetwode. Dated 12th March 1662.
(1662/3)   signed John Ashley
Wit. John Sharpe
      Stephen Chilton   Recorded 1st April 1663.

p. 257. Richard Merriman of Lanc., planter, sells to John Payne of the County of Rappa, planter, "my plantation whereon Mr Edward Dale now liveth and was heretofore demised unto the sd Edward Dale by the sd John Paine". Dated 6th Jan. 1662/3.   signed Richard Merryman
Wit. Will Blase
      Edward Dale   Rec. 14th May 1663.

p. 258. " Know all men by these presents that I Edward Waud Edward Waid Edward Ward Wardus"(sic) gives a heifer to Margaret Keeble.
Wit. Tho Kinge   signed Edward Ward (sic)
      Hen Herbert   Recorded 11th March 1662/3.

Note: Somebody else seems to have difficulty with simple names and to have finally fallen back on Latin. B.F.

p. 258. Robert Kempe, upon Sunderland Creek, in the parish of Lancaster in the County of Lancaster, planter, sells 300 acres to Joseph Smith and Humphrey Jones. Dated 13th May 1663. signed Robt Kempe
Wit. Will Nicholl
     Jos Pye
The consent of Elizabeth Kempe to above. signed Eliz Kempe.
                                  Recorded 13th May 1663.

p. 259. John Paine of Rappa., planter, sells to Richard Merryman of Lanc., planter,"all that plantation whereon Mr Edward Dale now liveth." Dated 6th February 1662/3.   signed   John Paine
Wit. Edward Dale
     Will Blayse

p. 260. Margaret Paine the wife of John Paine, consents to above and appoints "my trusty and well beloved friend Mr Edward Dale" atty to ack. sale. Dated 3rd March 1662/3.   signed   Margaret Paine
Wit. Robt Porke
     John Grave   Rec. 20th May 1663.

p. 260. John Simpson sells to Ennys Macenicee and Robert Rosse land being part of 600 acres he bought of Alex. Portous. Dated 4 May 1661
Wit. Will Stokes   signed   John Simpson
     Bryon Stott (Scott ?)   Ann Simpson
          Rec. 1st June 1661 (sic)
Memo. Robt Ross assigns land to Ennys Macenicee. Dated 13th May 1663.
Wit. Edward Dale   signed   Robt Ross
     Minor Doodes   Recorded 20th June 1663 (sic)

Note: The above name spelled Meconathey on page 212. B.F.

p. 261. Ennis Macenicee sells Robt Ross one half of above land bought by them from John Simpson. Dated 12th May 1663.
Wit. Minor Doodes   signed   Ennys Macenicee
     Edward Dale   Rec. 20 May 1663.

p. 261. Robt Ross sells Tho Maddeson his share of above land. Dated 13th May 1663.   signed   Robt Rosse
Wit. Edward Dale
     Ennys Macenicee   Rec. 20th May 1663.

p. 262. Ennys Macenicee sells his share of above to John Adamson . Dated 13th May 1663.   signed   Ennys Macenicee
Wit. Minor Doodes
     Edward Dale.   Rec. 20th May 1663.

p. 263. Mr. Cuth Potter of Rappa Co., in Virginia, merchant and Henry Ward, Marriner, appeared before Henry Corbyn, who had been authorized by Sir Wm. Berkeley "Collector of the Dutys of the sd Rappahannock" making oath that the "Galliet Hey" called the Henry and Mary was bought by them, the 10th of Sept last year from Alexander Danyson, Governor of Dellaware Bay. That "no one but Sir Henry Chicheley hath any part ownership in her". "None of the sd persons being aliens it is desired that the sd Galliet Hey may for the future be deemed as belonging to this port." Dated 20th April 1663.   signed Hen Corbyn Collector
Grant of above confirmed by Sir Wm. Berkeley 28th April 1663.

p. 263." A list of several bills belonging to John Jefferys Esq and Mr Thomas Colclough Mercht dd to Giles Cale by Samuel Griffin Vizt "

Anthony Stephens	830	Rich Peacocke	963
Tho Griffith	1026	Rich Cording	400
Jo Newman	3286	Will Bailey	43
Abratr Combes	206	Tho ffreshwater	411
Robt ffriste & Robt Turner	384	Jos Robbins	383
Colo Hen ffleete	214	Robt ffristo	827
Mrs Eliz Loes	555	Tho Staine	576
Geo Marsh	1806	Tho Chatwyn	3649
Tho Ludwell	1589	Hugh Daniel	441
Edward Lewys	2012	Nich Hugell	1000
Rich Powell	494	Nich Hugell to Hump Booth	921
James Webb	395	Hum Booth	1684
Nich Constable	22	Robt Bailey	1612
Robt Tomlyn	318	Jo Sherlow	516
Ja Sandford	495	Colo ffantleroy	636
Row Rowley	1774	Tho Masse Ralphe Warwicke	
Tho Chene	800	to Mr Corbyn	1250
Ciprian Bishop	56	Richd McKembill and Rich	
Tho Harding	394	Stephins to ditto	250
Rich Perrot	251	Hen Corbyn L 1.10	
Geo Hasleoke	610	Luke Billington	400
Widd Thackwell	48		- - - - - -
Robt Bidwell	108	Total tobo.	32785
Henry Olsen	150		

"Received of the hands of Mr Samuel Griffin the several bills above mentioned x x " Dated 1st June 1663.   signed   Giles Cale
Wit.   Robt Rogers
          Ambrose Cleare   Recorded 20th June 1663.

p. 264. "A list of several Bils bonds and notes dd to Giles Cale made and contracted per Nath Oxwitt decd in the names of Jo Jeffryes Esq and Mr Tho Colclough mercht   tobo

Rich Welby his bill	4824
Nich Cooke	409
Rich Cording	360
Edw Wauson	892
Clemt Herbert	649
Jo deYoung	117
Leonard Jones	107
Will Bawdos	160
Geo Colclough Isa ffoxcroft and	
Clemt Herbert jointly	1500
	- - - -
	9012

	a/c mony		
Hen Fleets bond	L 97.	10.	0
Edward Dales bill	13.	11.	11
Nich Cooke note	2.	11.	0
	- - - - - - - - - - - - -		
	113.	11.	11. "

This entry continued to next page.

Continued from previous page (#79)

"David ffoxs note a/c 1 case draws
Nich Cockes   "   "   "   "
Hen Corbyns note a/c 40 Ells canvas   12 perche hookes & 2 lynes

Recd of x x Mr Samuel Griffin the several bils bonds and notes above men-
tioned x x and oblige myselfe x x accountable to Jo Jeffreys Esq and Mr
Tho Cololough of London merchts x x x " Dated 1st June 1663.
Wit. Robt Rogers   signed Giles Cale
      Ambrose Cleare   Recorded 20th June 1663.

p. 265." A list of several bills recd of Mr Sam Griffin made in the name
of Mr Miles Dixon and others vizt

Nich Hale	849	Alex Porteus	265
Hen Hacker to Mr Jo		Richd Bowles	331
Jeffreys	245	Anth Jackman	311
Tho Willys	249	Jo Curtys	880
Toby Smiths a/c by		Edwyn Connoway to Mr	
Tho Pitman	751	Jo Jeffreys	1200
Dan Johnson	42	Tho Patteson	1409
Jo Washington	380		- - - - -
Tho Humphries	1555		8747
Tho Humphries a/c by			
Tho Griffith	380		

- - - - - - - - - - - - - - - - - -

Mr Geo Cololough	60.	0.	0
Will White assigned per ditto	10.	0.	0
Capt Sam Pensax	4.	0.	0
Isaac Foxcroft in 2 bills	6.	3.	6
Edm Kempe assigned per Matt Kempe	2.	0.	0
	- - - - - - - -		
	82.	3.	6

Recd of x x Mr Saml Griffin the several bills above mentioned x x and
oblige myself x x to be accountable to Jo Jeffreys Esq & Mr Tho Cololough
of London merchts x x " Dated 1st June 1663.
Wit. Robt Rogers   signed Giles Cale
      Ambrose Cleare   Recorded 20th June 1663.

Note: It must not be assumed that the persons whose names appear in the
above lists were all living at this date. Henry Fleet, for instance, had
died in the late spring of the year 1660. Doubtless others had passed on
that we do not know of. Beverley Fleet.

p. 265. "Acct of Bills & notes in the name of several men recd of Mr
Sam Griffin vizt
Will Johnson to Tho Griffin of London   344
Jacob Lumbroze (?) to Sam Chew for   260
a note of Tho Patteson to Mr Toby Smith   800
Dm Therriot to Capt Tho Thorogood   190
Mr Wm Underwood to Sam Groome   250
Tho Prettyman to Mrs Eliz Vaulx 2.15.0 Prettyman and
        Matt Kemp to Woodhouse 3.16.0
Edwd Kempe to Tho Stegge   697
Edwd Kempe to Tho Stegge per bills   1524
Sam Chew to Capt Hugh Wilson   900
Sam Chew to Richd Wright   250
John Meredith to Tho Thorogood   130
Jo Meredith to Tho Mann   300
Oliver Segar to Raw Travers   139
Anth Cheekes note to Jo Curtis per hhd tobo

    Recd of x x Mr Sam Griffin several bills above mentioned x x and oblige
myselfe to account to who they properly belong "   Dated 1st June 1663.
Wit. Robt Rogers   signed Giles Cale
      Ambrose Cleare   Recorded 22nd June 1663.

p. 266. "Virga June 2 1663
            Invoice of goods received of Sam Griffin being the remainder of
several cargoes which came into his hands as followeth"
            Then follows a long list of mdse with valuations in detail
amounting to L 168. 17. 1 . This list would be exceedingly interesting
to anyone who cared about the early trade betw. England and Virginia.

p. 267. Receipt to Sam Griffin. Dated 2nd June 1663.
Wit. Ambrose Cleare   signed Giles Cale
      Robt Rogers   Recorded 22nd June 1663.

p. 267. William Hutchings of Corotoman river, planter, sells to James
James 100 acres, being part of a patent dated June 1661 for 500 acres.
Dated 9th Sept 1663.   signed Will Hutchins
Wit. John Meredith   Rec. 10 Sept. 1663.

p. 267. Henry Nicholas of Lanc. Co., planter, gives to "my kindsman
David George one red cow x x" Dated 9th Sept 1663.
Wit. Robt Chowning   signed Hen Nicholas
      Moses Buffery   Rec. 14th Sept.1663.

p. 268. "I thomas Willyams & Martha Willyams my wife" sell to Will Pue
and Tho Widdower in Co. of Lanc., 100 acres "being backward part of a
dividend" belonging formerly to Evan Davys and Hen Nichols adj. land of
Richd White and Jo Welsh and also land of Tho Willys. Dated 17 Apl.1663.
Wit. Edw Roe   signed Tho Willyams
     Richd Lewys   Mar Willyams
                          Recorded 11th Sept 1663.

p. 268. Sir Henry Chicheley having purchased from John Jackson, of Lanc. lately decd, heir apparent of Capt. Will Brocas, likewise decd., 800 acres on S. side of Rappa., etc., as per Jackson's conveyance dated 13th Jan. 1656 (1656/7), sold this land to Will Bawde. Now Cuth Potter of Lanc., gent., Atty. for Sir Henry Chicheley, by virtue of Power of Atty. dated 24th Sept. 1661, for a valuable consideration to be paid to Chicheley, out of the Estate of Will Bawde, decd., according to the sd Bawde's obligation in his life time, sells, confirms, etc., to Mary Bawde, the daughter and heir of the sd Will Bawde, decd., the afsd. 800 acres. Dated 24 Sept 1663.
Wit. Matth Kompe   signed Cuth Potter
     Edward Dale   Recorded 28th Oct.1663.

p. 269. Thos Patteson of Co. of Rappa., planter, sells to Moses Baffery of Lanc., 200 acres on S. side of Rappa. Dated 12th Oct. 1663.
Wit. Edward Hopkinson   signed Tho Patteson
     Edward Hill   Ann Patteson
     Tho Belson   Rec. 20th Nov. 1663.

p. 270. Power of Atty. Tho Patteson and Ann Patteson to "our loving friend Mr Richd Perrot" of Lanc. Co., to ack above sale. Dat. 12th Oct. 1663.
                                         signed Tho Patteson
Wit. Edward Hopkinson   Ann Patteson
      Edward Hill
      Tho Belson   Rec. 11th Nov. 1663.

p. 270. Ellinor Owen of the County of Lanc., in Rappa. River, widow, for love and affection for her children, Olliver Segar, Randolph Segar and Ellinor Owen makes over household stuff and a negro to Mr. Richard Lee of the County of Rappa., planter, and Nicholas Cocke of the Co. of Lanc. Dated 30th Oct. 1663.   signed Elleanor Owen
Wit. John Haslewood   Recorded 20th Nov. 1663.

p. 271. Inventory of Olliver Segar and Humphrey Owen, their household goods, not a great deal, and "Item Five hundred acres of Land adjoining to Jamaica".   Recorded 20th Nov. 1663.

p. 272. "I Ellinor Owen of the County of Lancaster widow do give full order and power unto Mr Richd Perrot of the sd County gent to record this Deed of Gift to my children x x" Dated 9th Nov. 1663.
                                         signed Elleanor Owen
                                 Recorded 11th Nov. 1663.

p. 272. William Clappam of Lanc., planter, sells 780 acres, patented 20th Aug. 1650, to Mr. John Edwards of Lanc. Dated 14th Oct. 1663.
Wit. Tho Carter   signed Will Clappam
     Edward Dale   Rec. 20th Nov.1663.
Jane Clappam the wife of Will Clappam consents. Dated 11th Nov. 1663.
Wit. Richd Marshall   signed Jane Clappam
     John Haslewood   Rec. 20th Nov. 1663.

p. 273. John Edwards sells to Henry Davys 200 acres and agrees to make an ack of sale at next Court, and that his wife also do the like. Dated 14th Jan 1661/2. signed John Edwards
Wit. Geo fflower
 Jo fflower   Recorded 11th Nov. 1663.
 " I Eliza Chilton late the wife of John Edwards do freely consent to the sale of Land within mentioned x x" Dated 11th Nov. 1663.
Wit. Edward Dale   signed Eliza Chilton
     Recorded 20th Nov. 1663.

p. 273. Grant Sir William Berkeley to Mr. John Appleton, 1000 acres in Lanc. on S. side of Rappa., on N. side of the great swamp, lying N. from land of John Heyward, etc., this land formerly granted to Mr. Miles Dixon by patent dated 8th Dec. 1656 and now granted to Appleton. Dated at James City 15th May 1661. signed Will Berkeley
       Tho Ludwell Sec

  John Appleton of Lanc., mercht., sells above 1000 acres to Hen Ward of Lanc., marriner. Dated 11th Nov. 1663.
Wit. John Curtys   signed John Appleton
 Cuth Potter   Rec. 20th Nov. 1663.

p. 274. Re. a suit depending betw. Will Copeland, plaintiff and Richd Perrot, guardian of the children of Daniel Welsh, decd. 537 acres was sold by Welsh to Copeland. Perrot agrees to pay Copeland 2000 lb tobo and also to deliver to him his bill of 1500 lb of tobo from Capt Jennings, and to pay for the survey of the land. Copeland to have the land except what is "surveyed and taken away for the amount of Mr Rowland Burnham decd his children". Dated 16th July 1663. signed Richd. Perrott
Wit. Hen Corbyn   Will Copeland
 Tho Bowler   Recorded 20th Nov 1663.

p. 274. Indenture, 24th Nov. 1658, betw. Henry Corbyn of Lanc. in Va., gent., and Matth Kempe of the same Co., gent. Corbin sells Kempe 700 acres, hitherto belonging to Epaphroditus Lawson, decd., by patent, now or late in the hands of Will Clappam, junr., and late purchased by Corbin from Will Clappam. " x except reserved out of this grant Indenture unto Mr John Stephens x x x which neck of land is lying or being near unto another parcel of land x x x leased for a term of years yet to come x x unto Lt Colo Hon ffleete x x " signed Hen Corbyn
Wit. Ra Travers
 Cuth Potter "Recognit in cur 24 Nov Ano 1658 Recordat primo
    Decomb sequent"

p. 275. "I - - Kempe do hereby assign" right to above land to Mr. Robt Briggs, Warrenting the sd land to Robt Briggs from me Matthew Kempe and obliging myself that my wife Dorothy Kempe acknowledge the sd land x x"
Dated 2nd Sept. 1663   signed Matth Kempe
Wit. Grey Skipwith
 Edward Wyatt   Recorded 20th Dec. 1663.

p. 276. We, John Brueton and Christopher Withuel own and ack. joint ownership in certain property "and that interest in the Gallyet doth equally pertain and belong to us both." That the survivor shall be Exor. to the decd., "and dispose of it for the good of our friends in England". Dated 26th March 1663.   signed. Christopher Withuel
Wit. Robt Osburne   Jo Brueton
     Wm Downing   Rec. 20th Dec. 1663.

p. 276. Power of Atty. Dated "Yowocomico this 1 Jan (63) ". Richard Holden to "my good friend Joseph Chernell" to receive tobo due "within the County or Countys of Virginia".   signed Richd Holden
Wit. Wm Smyton (?)
     Willm Whitfeild   Recorded 13th Dec. 1663.

p. 277. Edward Bate gives to Sarah Blake certain items. John Blake also binds himself to this bill. No date shown.
Wit. Geo Mann   signed Edward Bate
     Tho Kinge   John Blake
                         Recorded 13th July 1664.

p. 277. Ennys Maconicoe (sic) records his mark for cattle and hogs.
No date.   No date of record.

p. 277. A calf recorded for Will the son of Will Emberson. Dated 10th Jan. 1663/4.   signed John Raney
Wit. Peter Elmore
     John Mott   No date of record shown.

p. 277. Nicholas Perquey, planter, in the County of Lancr. in Corotoman sells cattle to "Phillipa Squat daughter in law to the sd Perquey in London Living now & hath paid for the cows" before making the sale. Dated 8th July 1664.   signed Nich Perquey
Wit. Will Ironmunger
     Richd Kentish   Rec. 13th July 1664.

p. 277. John Appleton of Lanc., mercht., sells to Henry Ward of Lanc., marriner, for 7000 lb tobo, 1000 acres formerly patented by Mr Miles Dixon, decd., and "by him deserted and taken and patented by me the sd John Appleton". This land on S. side of Lanc. Co., adj land of John Haward, etc. Dated 1st May 1664.   signed Jo Appleton
Wit. Jo Dixon
     Edw Dale   Rec. 20 Jul 1664.

p.278. Henry Ward of Lanc., sells Rice Jones of Lanc., 1000 acres for
8000 lb tobo. Dated 10th May 1664.   signed Hen Ward
Wit. John Appleton
      Edward Dale   "recognit 13 July 1664"

p. 280. Robt Kendall agrees to pay George Marsh 1500 lb tobo, 10th Oct.
next at the plantation of John Haslewood. Dated 30th May 1664.
Wit. Richd Perrot   signed Robt Kendall
     Tho Warwick   "Recognit 13th July 1664"

p. 280. Robt Kendall agrees to pay Geo Marsh 1000 lb tobo 10th Oct.1665
"or at the day of my death" Dated 30th May 1664.
Wit. Richd Perrot   signed Robt Kendall
     Tho Warwick   Recorded 20th July 1664.

p. 281. To secure foregoing bills amounting to 2500 lb tobo, Robt.
Kendall assigns to Geo Marsh. crop to be made this year upon plantation
of John Haslewood, one cow and one yearling upon plantation of Mr Richd
Perrot, one feather bed and boulster, one rug and two blankets.
Dated 30th May 1664.   signed Robt Kendall
Wit. Richd Perrot
     Tho Warwick   Recorded 20th July 1664.

p. 281. Grant ffran Morryson, Esq., to John Ashley 240 acres. Dated at
James Citty 10th June 1662.   signed ffran Morryson
                                                Tho Ludwell
     " I do assign all my right title and Interest of this patent with-
in mentioned unto (Part of page missing here) his heirs or assgs forever
x x my wifes acknowledgemt as x x x of July 1664 "
                                        signed Tho Chetwode
                                Recorded 20th July 1664.
p. 282. Power of Atty. Eliz Chetwode to Mr.Henry Hazlewood to ack to
Magno Barret "my right in a tract of land wch my husband hath sold the
sd Barret." Dated 12th July 1664.   signed Eliz Chetwode
Wit. John Simpson
      John Brenniard   Recorded 20th July 1664.

p. 282. Power of Atty. "Joseph Hunt of the Citty of Bristol mercht" to
"my trusty & well beloved friend Hugh Brent of ffleets Bay in the County
of Lanc planter" to collect debts. Dated 20th Aug. 1663.
Wit. Mich Hunt   signed Joseph Hunt
     Tho Medor (?)
     Geo Grigson junr   Date recorded missing-page torn away.

p. 283. Bill of Will Hutchins of Corotoman in Co. of Lanc.,planter to
Emanuel Ewery of the City of Bristol, Marriner, for 2640 lb tobo payable
10th Oct. next. This name spelled again as Everey. Security for this bill
a servant man called Geo Henson, crop, etc. Dated 7th June 1664.
Wit. Hugh Brent   signed Will Hutchins
      Will Thacker   Recorded 13th July 1664.

p. 283. "To all to whom these presents shal come Greeting in our Lord God everlasting Know yee that I David Fox of the county of Lancast in Rappa River in Virga Gent as wel for the natural Love & affection woh I bear unto my children Davyd Fox and Hannah Fox as also for divers other good causes & considerations me thereunto moving have given granted and aliened bargained sold infeoffed & confirmed & do by these presents for me my heirs Exors & Admr give grant alion bargain sell enfeoff & confirm unto my Loving friends Capt Thomas Carter & Mr Edward Dale of the County of Lancast in Rappah river in Virga Gent all those Lands goods & chattels cattle monys negroes English servts horses sheep household stuff & implomts of household and all other my estate x x x to the use & behoof of me the sd Davyd Fox during my natural life & after my decease to the use & behoof of my sd children Davyd Fox & Hannah Fox & their heirs Exers admr & asss forever according to the division in the sd schedule expressed & to no other use or uses intents or purposes whatsoever & I the sd Davyd Fox have put the sd Capt Tho Carter & Mr Edward Dale in possession of all the premisses by the delivery of a gold ring part of the per- - in the name of seizen In witnes whereof I have hereunto put my hand & seale this fourteenth day of Sept 1664"

Wit. Dno Therryott   signed Davyd ffox
Tho Chetwode

p. 284. "For my son Davyd Fox Anthony Alkamy Cooper Congo Guy James Acorue Robin Sisly Katherine 10 negroes Thirty head of old cattle being twenty cows and ten steers fforty ewes and one ram one grey gelding six pr of new holland sheets & six pr of new holland pillow beers two feather beds wth bolster pillows blankets rugs curtains & vallains thereunto belonging six turkey worke chairs two Iron potts all monys sterl: that I have in England being in the hands of Mr Jo Jeffrys & Mr Tho Cololough merchants in London as per their accot currt of the 24th of Octob: 1663 doth appear except one hundred pds thereof wch I give unto my daughter Hannah ffox all my land lying & being on the north side of Rappah: river due to me by patent or otherwise together wth all houses edefices & building thereunto belonging But in case of his mortality or want of due heirs by him Lawfully begotten then successively to fall to my daughter Hannah Fox & eight large pewter dishes (sic)

   " For my daughter Hannah Fox One negro man called ffrancis & all the negro children one hundred pounds sterl: twenty ewes & a ram one new feather bed wth boulston pillows blankets ruggs curtains and vallains six pr of new holland sheets & six pr of new holland pillowcases four large pewter dishes all the wearing apparell that belonged to my dead wife Mrs Mary ffox being as followeth vizt one flowered sattin corderobe one clothsilver waist coate one new black lutestring gown & petty coate one new sky collourd sattin pettycoat one new Lemmon tabley colloured pettycoat one new black taffaty pettycoat one scarlet cloth pettycoat wth a parchmt lace one bodye wth a parchmt lace one scarlet bay pettycoat wth a smal lace one body serge pettecoat two new one old straw coloured flannel pettycoats two straw coloured waistcoats being flannel one body wastcoat laced wth a silver lace one grey silk pettycoat one red pettycoat one red riding suite one colord serge suit wth a silver lace one womans scarlet cloake one pr of scarlet sattin boddice one pair of white sattin boddice one pr of white sarsnet boddice one pr of Lemon colourd tabby boddice one pr of Lemon colourd silke stockings "   signed Davyd ffox
Recorded 14th Sept. 1664.

p. 285. John Curtys of Lanc., solls, for L 154. sterl: pd by Tho Bowler, mercht., 6 English servants and 6 negro women "named as followeth Willm Hoy Hugh Williams Tho Price Tho Peirce Jo Watson & Tho Reynolds Diana Jone ffranke Juno Anne Maria x x x the sd negroes formerly bought of Tho Bowler." Dated 7th May 1664.
Wit. Tho Harwar   signed Jo Curtys
     John Sergeant   Rec. 20th Sept 1664.

p. 286. Jo Curtys of Lanc., gent., sells to Will Downing of the same County, Taylor, 300 acres adj. "Davyd Allysons seat of land." Dated 20th July 1664.   signed Jo Curtys
Memo. Ann Curtys the wife of Jo Curtys consents and authorizes Robert Osburne to ack. this in Court. Date as above.
Wit. Peter Chavanne   signed Ann Curtys
     William Haighe   Rec. 20th Sept 1664.

p. 287. Will Hutchins of Corotoman sells 50 acres and 300 acres to Alexander Reade of the same Co. Deed refers to "the sd Hutchins & Eliz his wife." Dated 2 Feb. 1663/4.   signed Will Hutchins
Wit. Geo fflower   Eliz Hutchins
     Walter Herd
Power of Atty. Eliz Hutchins "to my loving friend Jo Walker" to ack sale.
Dated 14th Sept 1664.   signed Eliz Hutchins
Wit. Will Thatcher
     Geo Hanson   Recorded 20th Sept. 1664.

p. 288. Jo Jadwin of Lanc., planter, lets to Will Cheyney and Margt his wife, 100 acres, the term of their lives. Also 5 cows and 2 breeding sows, the sd Will Cheyney adding the like number of cattle, etc., and he to look after the stock. Dated 12th Sept. 1664.
Wit. Will Thompson   signed Jo Jadwyn
     James Blackmore   Will Cheyney
                              Rec. 20th Sept.1664.

p. 289. John Jadwyn of Lanc., lets to Domingo Bras (Cras) land adj. Will Blayse and Will Thompson. Domingo to let Will Cheyney have, for the next year, as much corn and ground as will hold 1500 corn holes, and also 15 ft. of the 50 ft. tobo house. Domingo to let the tobacco ground Hen Piggott has cleared alone. Jadwyn and Domingo to each put in stock and divide the profits. Lease for term of 10 years. Dated 6th Oct.1664.
Wit. Tho Smith   signed Jo Jadwyn
     Peter Montague   Domingo Bras
                              Rec. 20th Sept. 1664.
Power of Atty. Jo Jadwyn to Hump Jones to ack. the above two leases in Court.   signed "Yr Lo friend
                                              Jo Jadwyn "
                              Rec. 20th Sept. 1664.

p. 291. "Barbados . . . Know all men that I Jo Barwick of the Island
above Mercht x x x appoint my lo friend Isaac Hill of the sd Island
Mercht to be my Lawful Attorney x x" to collect debts and transact
other business. Dated 30th July 1664. signed Jo Barwick
Wit. John Canaway   Robt Jordan
     Geo Norton   Tho Walke

p. 291. Power of Atty. 23rd Aug. 1664. "x x before me Frederick Ixom
sole notary x x There appeared Thurston Withuell of London Mercht being
as he declared natural brother heir & principal creditor of Christopher
Withuell late of Virginia Mercht decd ". He appoints Cuth Potter & Robt
Osborne of Va., planters, his attorneys to collect from John Bructon of
Virginia, planter, etc.   signed Thurston Withuell
Wit. Will Hall
      Ja - - - -
      Will - - -
      Robt Barton   Rec. 9th Nov. 1664.

p. 292. Nicholas Cocke desires that cattle be recorded for Charles
Bridgar (sic) the son of Richd Bredgar (sic). No date.
                              signed Nich Cocke
                         Rec. 9 Nov. 1664.

p. 293. Thomas Powell of Lanc., gent., "for natural love and affection I
bear to Mrs Jane Catesby whom I intend suddenly (God willing) to make my
wife" gives the money, stock and land that is here specified, viz. 200
pounds sterling etc. Dated 2 Oct. 1664. signed Tho Powell
Wit. Davyd ffox
     Geo Vezey
     John Dawe (?)   Recorded 20th Nov. 1664.

p. 293. Power of Atty. Eliz Hutchins to John Meredith to ack sale of 300
acres and 50 acres to Alexander Reade. Dated 8th Nov. 1664.
Wit. Walter Herd   signed Eliz Hutchins
     Tho Dellahay   Recorded 20th Nov. 1664.

p. 294. Adry Hill gives to Christopher Kilby a cow calf. Dated 1st Apl.
1660.   signed Adry Hill
Wit. Enock Boome
     Jo Boorman   Recorded 9th Nov. 1664.

p.294. Richard Lewys of Lanc., planter, sells to Will Pue of the same
Co., planter, for L 10. sterl:, 200 acres adj land of Robt Kempe, John
Blueford, Mr. Robt Chowning, etc. Dated 2nd Dec. 1664.
Wit. Jo Vause   signed Richard Lewys
     Anne Vause   Recorded 1st Jan 1664.

p. 295.   2nd Aug. 1663. There came before John Daniell, notary, etc in London, Richard Longman of London, mercht., who appoints Thomas James, "Comander of the ship Duke of Yorke" his attorney to collect debts in Rappa. River in Va.   signed Rich Longman
Wit. John Nelson   Jo Daniell Notarius Pub.
      Archibald Cunningham   Rec. 14th Dec. 1664.

p. 296. Thos. Chetwode of Lanc., sells to Magne Barret 240 acres "and with the consent of his wife". Her name not shown. Dat.2nd Apl. 1664.
Wit. John Wortham   signed Tho Chetwode
      Hugh Jordan   Rec. 14th Dec. 1664.

p. 296. Grant from Sr Wm Berkeley to Will Clappam, 700 acres. Of this 300 acres formerly granted to William Clappam junior, 15th Sept. 1651 and by him assigned to Tho Powell, this 300 a. adj. land of Anthony Doney. Also 400 acres adj. land of afsd. Tho Powell, also adj. land of Capt. Tho Hackett, this 400 a. formerly granted to Tho Powell 8th June 1658 and by him assigned to Will Clappam. Dated James Citty 11th Dec. 1663.
Wit. Fra Kirkman   signed Will Berkeley

p. 297. Will Clappam of Lanc., planter, sells to Edward Dale of the same County, Gentleman, the above 700 acres, excepting 350 acres assigned to Jno Berry. Dated 14th Dec. 1664. signed Will Clappam
Wit. Richd Lawrence
      Giles Cale   Rec. 1st Jan. 1664/5.

Power of Atty. Jane Clappam to Mr. Geo fflower to ack above sale.
Dated Jan. 6th 1664/5.   signed Jane Clappam
Wit. Willm Smith
      Robt ffarrington   Rec. 20th Jan 1664/5.

p. 298. "Mr fflower Pray record these two cows for my daughter Mary two red cows called by name Cherry and Rose and their increase marked wth two half moons under each ear and one half spade upon each ear to be recorded for Mary Clappam aged about 4 or 5 years" No date.
Wit. Will Smith   signed Will Clappam
      Robt ffarington   Recorded 20th Jan 1664/5.

p. 298. James Citty, Dec. 31st 1664. Thos Loving, Surveyor General of Virginia , appoints Mr. Thomas Chetwode "Surveyor of all the land in Lancaster County on the north side of Rappahannock x x"
                                signed Tho Loving
                                Recorded 11th Jan. 1664/5.

p. 299.   Bill of Jo Merrideth,Boatwright, of Lanc., to John Carter of
Lanc., 6008 lb. tobo. to be paid on or before 10th Nov. next, at John
Meredith's dwelling plantation. "Always provided that 2700 lb tobo of
the sd debt is for a note of security of 900 lb. tobo passed by the sd
John Carter to Mr Tho Bowler and another note of security of 900 lb of
tobo to Mr Travers also for another note of security to Mr Kentish to
Mr James x x x the sd John Meredith or his assigns bring any of the sd
notes to the sd John Carter x x" that he is thereby discharged from the
sd security before the 10th of Nov. Security given for this indebtedness,
plantation, 3 men and 1 maid servants, named Jo Jones, Xtopher Etty,
Will Waller and Eliz West. Also other items, crop, cattle, etc.
Dated 21st Dec. 1664.   signed John Meredith
Wit. Pierre Mage
      William Pitcher   Rec. 20 Jan. 1664/5.

p. 299. Jo Curtys of Lanc., gent., sells to John Smith of same Co, planter, 300 acres adj. land of Mr. Cuth Potter, Davyd Allyson, etc. Smith
being now and for one year past seated upon this land. Curtis obliges himself that "my now wife" sall confiem this. Dated 11th Jan.1664/5.
Wit. Cuth Potter   signed Jo Curtys
      Edward Dale   Rec. 20th Jan 1664/5.

p. 300. Will Clappam of Corotoman in Lanc., sells to Arthur Branch of
Wiccocomoco in the County of Northumberland, half of a div. of 530
acres purchased from Geo. Taylor. "The sd Clappam & Jane his wife do
hereby engage themselves to make ack. x x of the sale x ". Dat.6 Jan.1664.
Wit. George fflower   signed Will Clappam
      Will Smith   Jane Clappam
      Robt ffarington   Rec. Jan. - - 1664/5.

p. 301. Sir Wm. Berkeley grants to Thomas Chetwode, gent., 200 acres.
Dated James Citty, 9th July 1663.   signed William Berkeley
                                             Tho Ludwell Secr
"Mr Tho Chetwode his Patt for 250 acr of land
                            Test Fra Hickoman "
Tho. Chetwode assigns above to John Chinly and also makes ack for his
wife. Dated 17th August 1664.   signed Tho Chetwode
Wit. Jno Sympson
      Bryan Stott (Scott ?)   Rec. 8th Feb 1664/5

p. 301. Will Hutchins having formerly sold to James James 100 acres,
James for a consideration received from Hutchins, re assigns his interest
to him. Dated 8th Feb. 1664/5.   signed Ja James
Wit. Tho Madestard
      Reuben Fisher   Rec. 8th Feb. 1664/5.

p. 302. Memo. Robt Swann of London, marriner, appoints Mr. Will Neesham of Lanc. Atty., to ack. sale of 350 acres to Edward Lunsford. Dated 23rd Jan. 1664/5.   signed Robert Swann
Wit. Ben Whiscom
      Edward Dale   Recorded 8th Feb. 1664/5.

p. 302. Robt Swann of London, marriner, sells Edward Lunsford of the Co. of Rappa. in Virginia, planter, 350 acres now in the occupation of the sd Lunsford, formerly patented by John Jones and by Jones deserted and taken by Thos Chetwode and by Chotwode assigned to Will Wroughton, and by Will Wroughton assigned to the above sd. Robt Swann. Dated 1 Jan. 1664/5.
Wit. Ben Whiscom   signed Robt Swann
      Edward Dale   Rec. 8th Feb. 1664/5.

p. 303. Edward Lunsford of Lanc., planter, sells above 350 acres to Edw. Dale of the same Co., gentleman. Dated 2 Feb. 1664/5.
Wit. Cuth Rynes   signed Edi Lunsford (sic)
      Will Neesum   Rec. 10th Feb. 1664.

p. 304. "I do give Mr Jo Curtys lycence to survey for himself 3 or 4 thousand acres of land lying upon Nansattico & Nansamon dated the 28th of Jan 1664   signed Tho Chetwode   "
                              Rec. 1st March 1664/5.

p. 304. Hen Reeves of the Isle of Wight Co., planter, Admr. to the Estate of Robt. Sharpe, junr., late of the County of Rappa., decd., appoints Edward Dale of the Co. of Lanc., gent., Atty. to receive money, papers, etc. from Capt. Janisar Plover. Dated 21st Feb. 1664/5
Wit. Rich Merryman   signed Hen Reeves
      Elleanor Nichols   Rec. 24th Feb. 1664/5.

p. 305.   13th Oct. 1664. Frederick Ixom, notary in London, states: "There personally appeared Sarah Higginson wife of Samuel Higginson of Lymehouse in the County of Middx marriner & declared that whereas her sd husband by Letter of Attorney under his hand & seale bearing date the third day of August 1661 hath x x constituted her x x his attorney & deputy x x that by reason of her other affairs cannot transport herself to Virginia & doth hereby make & ordain in her stead William Hall of London marrinor her law-ful attorney to receive sums of money etc owing & belonging to sd Saml Higginson by persons in Virginia"   signed Sarah Higginson
Wit. Edmond Sheldon
      Charles Goldston
"Edmond Sheldon and Charles Goldston were this day sworn before me x x x they were present & saw Sarah Higginson seal & deliver the within written Letter of Attorney x x" Dated May 12th 1665.
                              signed Hen Corbyn
                              Recorded 20th May 1665.

p. 306. Richard Gower, John Miller, Will Howson, James Holland, John Stone
and Hugh Noden, all of London, merchants, appoint Mr. Will Hall, Commander
of the ship Providence and Mr James Sumpner (?) or either of them attorneys
to collect debts etc., in Va., due on cargoes sent last year and consigned to the sd. Will Hall and James Sumpner and to Mr Leonard Howson.
Dated 22 Oct. 1664.   signed Rich Gower   James Holland
Wit. Rich Morrys   Jo Miller   John Stone
     Edmon Sheldon   Will Howson   Hugh Noden
     Tho Johnson

   "Edmond Sheldon this day did swear before me that he saw the several
persons x x sign seal and deliver the within written Letter of Attorney"
Dated May 12th 1665.   signed Hen Corbyn
                              Recorded 20th May 1665.

p. 307. "A list of several Bills for tobo and Bills of Exchange left in
the hands of Mr Cuth Potter by Will Hall for his own use and for several
other persons hereafter signified May the 27th 1665 vizt
One bill of Mr Raw Travers being payable to Mr Rich Gower   8504
                 Payable to Mr Hall
#1   a bil of Mr Tho Glascocke for   3743
 2   A bil of Mr Geo Wale for   1840
 3   A bil of Mr Will Travers   1576
 4   An ingagemt of Colo Goodriche   904
 5   A bil of Peter Bacomes (?)   400
 6   an engagemt of Mr Ra Travers   284
 7   a note of Mr Ball for   50
 8   a rect for a seale ring of white stone wth a death head   . . .
 9   a bil of Hen Ware & Hen Haslewood is an accot   112
10   Goody Bond bil for the owners   115
11   a bil of Abraham Weekes payable to Will Hall   740
               Upon the acct of Mrs Sarah Higginson
A bil made payable to Will Hall from John Ellix of Wicoocomocoe 1000
a bil of Mr Hum Booths   1077
a bil in the hands of Mr John Hull of Denbeigh for   1888
A bil of Dudloes (Dudley's ?) for   100
A bil of Will Young payable to James Goodman   728

             Bills of Exchange payable to Will Hall left
                       wth Mr Potter
a bill drawn by Edmond Sheldon for   L 2.12.0
a bill drawn by Marke Grayne   6.16.0
a bill drawn by Mr Robt Baynard & Mr Dan Bradley   4.00.0
a bill drawn by Charles Hutchins   17.04.0

An Invoice of goods left in the hands of Mr Ra Travers
      May the 26th 1664 is his ingagemt to be accountable
      for the sd goods to Mr Rich Gower & Company   15.11.9

"I underwritten Cuth Potter do acknowledge to have recd the above x x x
     Bills x x"   signed Cuth Potter
Wit. Rich Robinson
     James Mills   Recorded 29th May 1665.

p. 309. " Recd this presnt 27th of May 1665 one sloop and sixteen foot
flat bottomed boat wth 2 oars riggd and fitted vizt a mainsale x x which
sloop boat and rigging belongs to the ship Providence all which I do hereby promse to secure and keep safe and to deliver unto the sd Will Hall or
his order upon his or their demand " signed Cuth Potter
Wit. Robt Beverley
     Rich Robinson   Recorded 29th May 1665.

p. 309. "Recd Mr Will Hall the sum of three thousand pounds of tobo and
recd for the hire of two sloops three months for the use of the ship
Providence as also 840 lb tobo and recd for 560 foot of Inch & halfe
plank wch was for the use of the sd ship I say recd this 27th of May
1665"   signed Cuth Potter
Wit. Rich Robinson
     Robt Beverloy   Recorded 29th May 1665.

p. 309. "An acct stated of what is due to Mr Jo Campian by me Rich
Merryman the 14th Augt 1661 "
Account includes:
1664 Sent this year by Mr Hall as followeth as per notes
         and accts of Mr Jo Campian
         Mr Huttons note for 27 bushels of mault   2.14.3
         Mr Campian his own note of disbursemts   8.16.8
         Mr Mathews note for clothing of 3 servts & other goods13. 7.8
         For the passage of 3 servts & head money   18.15.0
                                    - - - - -

The total of the account amounts to L 344.0.2

p. 310. "These may certify whom it may concern that is a true copy of
all accts between Mr Jo Campian Pewterer of London and Richard Merryman
of Virginia Planter from the year of our Lord 1661 to 23rd of Octob 1664
certified by me Rich Hall being the true and lawful attorney of the aforsd
John Campian as witness my hand this 20th of May 1665"
                    signed Will Hall (sic)
                    Recorded 27th May 1665.
Note: The name Rich Hall evidently appears in the above in error. The name
should be Will Hall. B.F.

p. 310. Richard Merryman of Lanc. Co., Rappahannock River in Virginia,
planter, to John Campian of London, pewterer. Refers to "one pair of
Indentures bearing date the 25th of Decemb 1663". These to remain in full
force as of this date. Parts of this record in Latin. Involved and difficult to decipher.   signed Richd Merryman
Wit. Edward Dale
     Tho Kendall   Recorded 29th May 1665.

p.310.   Goods of Mr Rich Gower consigned to Mr Potter
To 36 yds of red cotton at 21 d pr yd   3.   0.   6
To 50 Ells of Canvas at 15 d per Ell   3. 12.   6
          etc. x x x

                                            - - - - - - -
                    Total   28.   6. 11

          Goods of Mr James Holland consigned to Mr Potter
To 9 doz of stockings at 14 d per Doz   6.   6.   0
          etc. x x x

                                            - - - - - - -
                    Total   33.   5.   0

          Goods of Mr Will Hall consigned to Mr Potter
To 18 yds of black cotton at 18 d per yd   1.   7.   0
          etc. x x x

                                            - - - - - - -
                    Total   10.   9.   7

        "I Cuth Potter do ack to have rec of Willm Hall the several goods
above mentioned x x this 20th day of May 1665 x x "
Wit. Rich Robinson   signed Cuth Potter
     Tho Chetwode   Recorded 20th May 1665.

p. 312. "Raw Travers of the County of Lancast Mercht do acknowledge that
I have recd of Will Hall the within mentioned bills amounting to 12472
lb tobo for use of Mr Rich Gower & Company the sd bills were delivered to
the sd Hall and James Sumpner by Mr Leo Howson x x." Dated 26th May 1665.
Wit. Will Travers   signed Raleigh Travers
     Gregory Glascocke   Recorded 29th May 1665.

p. 312. "A list of Bills and ingagemts left in the hands of Mr Cuth
Potter by Mr Will Hall May the 30th 1665 & also goods
#1 To Thos Gaskins bill to Will Hall accounts by Richd Browne   2000
 2 to Mr Corbyns bil to Will Hall for   2800
 3 to Will Lennells bil to Will Hall for   394
        to Mr Jo Appletons ingagement to a list of several things
left in the hands of Mr Rich Merryman to Rich Merrymans rect and
acknowledgment of sale of 1000 acres of Land to a bill of Exch:
of Mr Bradshaws for fourteen pounds sterl to 2 suits of Cloths all
moth eaten belonging to Mr Bower servts hath been 2 years in Virga
left wth Mr Potter to get what he can for them
        A woolsted work petticoat belonging to Mr Howson   L 1. 4. 0

        The several things above mentioned I underwritten do acknowledge
to have recd of Mr Willm Hall "   Dated 30th May 1665.
Wit. Rich Robinson   signed Cuth Potter
      John Watson
                         Recorded 30th May 1665.

p. 313.   Geo Keeble sells to Peter Rigby land "being in Pieankitank".
Refers to "my wife Mary Keeble". Dated 18th Jany 1657/8.
Wit. Jo Curtys   signed Geo Keeble
      Jo Humphreys   Mary Keeble
"Know all men by these presents that I Thomas Hill of Pieankitank in the
County of Lancaster do assign all my right and title of this bill from me
my heirs Exors and assgs unto Will: Dudley of the same county his heirs
Exors and assigns forever as witness my hand this 28th of Jan 1664"(1664/5)
Wit. Geo Mann   signed Thomas Hill
      Hen Herbert   Recorded 1st June 1665.
" Mr Dale   I would intreat you to acknowledge this bill of sale in Court
unto Mr Will Dudley and this my note shal impower you as much as if I my-
selfe were there present"   signed Tho Hill
Wit. Geo Mann
      Hen Herbert   Recorded 10th day May 1665 (sic)

p. 314.   Moses Buffery of Lanc., planter, sells to Edmond Mickleborough
of the same Co., planter, for ten pounds sterl., 200 acres lying upon
Burnhams Creek, etc. Dated 16th Feb. 1664/5.
Wit. Robt Chowning   signed Moses Buffery
      Geo Colings   Rec. 1st June 1665.

p. 315." I underwritten do ack to have recd of Mr Will Hall an anchor
weighing 460 lb it being for the ship Berkeley x x to be delivered upon
the arrival of the ship Berkeley in the river of Thames or that Mr Gawyn
Corbyn shal buy a new one of the same weight & deliver unto the sd Hall
In confirmation of I have hereunto set my hand this 30th of May 1665"
Wit. Rich Robinson   signed Cuth Potter
      John Watson   Recorded 30th May 1665.

p. 315.   John Curtys of Lanc., gent., sells to George Vosey & Nathanl
Brown of the Co of Lanc., planters, 400 acres at hte head of Morattico
Creek, adj. land of Jo Newman, etc. Dated 1st March 1664/5.
Wit. Rich Merryman   signed Jo Curtys
      Edward Dale   Recorded 1st April 1665.

p. 317.   Will Ironmonger of Lanc., planter, sells to Geo fflower of Lanc.,
mercht., for forty pounds sterl., 2 men servants named Peter Shaw and Jo
Meryfeild wth all their crop of corn and tobo "they shall make upon the
plantation of the sd Ironmonger in the river of Corotoman." Agrees to
protect Flower in regard to a jdgmt. to pay 4000 lb tobo, on 20th Nov.
next, to Mr Jo Edwards. Dated 28th Feb. 1664/5.
Wit. Tho Marshall   signed Wm Ironmonger
      Rich Kentish

                                     Recorded 1st June 1665.

p. 318. Grant of ffrancys Morryson, Esq., to Mr. George Wale, 1400 acres bounded as followeth, vizt. 600 acres x x on the S. side of a creek issuing out of ffleets bay called Corotoman Creek, being the next creek northerly to Haddaways Creek, bounding S.E. upon a tract of land formerly surveyed for Toby Horton, by some called Mr Wetherbys land, N.E; upon the sd creek from the sd land to the head of the main branch thereof, S.W. upon the land of Jo Taylor, decd., N.W. upon the main woods. And 300 acres other part thereof situate near the glade above Wicc- - - - Indian Town, joining to the south side of the land of Jo Cosens and Tho Steede (?) x x x to another belonging to the sd Wale by assignment from Geo Dodson x x x bounding upon the land of Gervase Dodson, further bounding upon land formerly granted to Gervase Dodson, by patent dated 3rd March 1656 (1656/7) and 500 acres other, likewise formerly granted to sd Dodson by patent dated 29th Nov. 1658 and by sd Dodson assigned to sd Wale.
Dated at James Citty 10th Oct.1662.   signed ffrancys Morryson
                                                 Tho Ludwell Sec

    Goe Wale sells to Tho Hains part of above and says "that Lewys my wife" consents to sale. Dated 11th Jan. 1664/5.
Wit. Robt Jones   signed Geo Wale
     Hen Houghton   Lewys Wale (Lois ?)
                          Recorded 1st June 1665.

p. 320. "Know all men by these presents that we George Wale and Lewys Wale wife of the sd Geo Wale do by these presents authorize and ordaine our loving brother Edward Wale our true and lawful attorney" x x to ack above sale to Tho Haines. Dated 9th May 1665.
Wit. Tho Jenner   signed Geo Wale
     Robt Huff (Hull ?)   Lewys Wale
                          Recorded 10th May 1665

p. 320. "Charles the son of Teage Correll was borne Jan the 30 1660
Abraham the son of Teage Correll was borne Septemb the 18th 1662
Teage Carroll recordeth for his son Abraham one red cow 2 years old wth calfe marked vizt cropt on both ears one slit in the right ear & a - - - in the left
    Isaac the son of Teage Correll was borne May the 4th 1664
    Teage Correll recordeth for his son Isaac one cow red & white cropt on boath ears & two slits in each ear "
                          Recorded 1 June 1665
" Teage Correll recordeth for Charles his son two cows both cropt on the right ear & a slit in the left ear wth a cow calfe of the same marke"
                          Recorded 1 June 1665

p. 321. Bill binding Henry Corbyn of Lanc., to pay 1030 lb tobo to Rice Hill 10th day of Nov. next. Dated 29th May 1665.
Wit. John Appleton   signed Hen Corbyn
     Hum Clerke
                          Recorded 13th July 1665.

p. 321. "Virga the first of June 1665.
At ten days after sight this my third bil of Exch: my first and second
not being paid x x x unto Mr Will Hall or his order the sum of two pounds
three shillings Sterl mony wch is for Virga Import at the time make good
paymt and place to acco as per advice of
To Capt Junifer Plower in Lower   Your serv
Shadwell near Bell Wharfe near   Tho Madestard
London

          Virga the first of June 1665.
     The second bil of Exch of the same tenor
To Capt Junifer Plower in Lower   Tho Madestard
Shadwell near Bell Wharf near
London. "   Recorded 12th 1665.

p. 321. Bill of Cuth Potter of Lanc., merch., to Mr. Will Hall for 3060
lb tobo on or before 20th Nov. next. Dated 30th May 1665.
Wit. Rich Robinson   signed Cuth Potter
      John Watson   Rec. 12 Jul. 1665.

p. 321. "Ten days after sight this my first bil of Exch: my second and
third not paid pay unto Mr Cuth Potter or his order the sum of six pounds
ten shillings x x the like value here received of him at the time make
good payment & place to the acco of   Your Lov Brother
                                        Richard Bushrode
Dated in Virga ffobr 22 1664
To my Lov Brother Mr Mark Workeman
at the Kings Armes in the old Change in London

          A second bill of the same tenor subscribed & directed as above sd"
                    Recorded 12 Jul 1665.

p. 322. Hugh Kinsey sells John ffish of London, ffletcher, 500 acres for
L 33.6.8 Sterl. to be paid 25th of Jan. following. Dated 24th May 1662.
Wit. Mylos Ryley   signed Hugh Kinsey
     Edward Dale   Rec. 1st Aug. 1662. (sic)

p. 322..   "We Will Neasum and Edmond ffaroe attorneys of Mr Jo ffish of
London mercht as well as for and in consideration of thirty and four
pounds sterl in hand paid by bill of Exch recd of Wm Capell of London
Cooper sell to sd Will Capel all that plantation within montioned"
Dated 9th April 1663.   signed Will Neasum
Wit. Edw Dale   Edm ffaroe
     Eliz Turner   Rec. 1st Aug. 1665.

p. 323. John ffish citizen and ffletcher of London. "whereas my attorney
Edmond ffaroe of Wapping in the County of Middx marriner and Will Neasum
of Virginia planter did by authority by me granted sell to Will Capell
citizen and coopor of London one plantation situate in Lancashire in the
sd Country of Virginia wch was mortgaged and forfieted unto me by one
Hugh Kensey of Virga afsd planter"   Dated 29th June 1663.
Wit. Robt Casby   signed Jo Fish
     Hen Clerke
     Sam Griffin   Rec. 1st Aug.1665.

p.323. "According to the tenor of this bil of sale I have surveyed for Roger Kelley 400 acres x x being part of a divident of 1200 acres x x "
signed Tho Chetwode
Teage Correll sells to Roger Kelley the 400 acres above. Dat.13 Sept.1665.
Wit. Tho Medestard   signed Teage Corroll
     Hugh Brent   Rec. 13th Sept. 1665.

p. 324. Abraham Bush of Lanc. sells to Hubert Patey 150 acres. Dated 9th Sept. 1665.   signed Abraham Bush
Edward Williams
Tho Chetwode   Rec. 1st Oct. 1665

p. 324. Robert Gorsuch and Rich Gorsuch sell to Ralph Horton 600 acres. Refers to Tho Powell as attorney for Robt. Gorsuch. Dated 27 Feb. 1664/5.
Wit. Edw Roe   signed Rich Gorsuch
     Howell Powell   Tho Powell
            Rec. 1st Oct. 1665.
    Power of Atty. Rich Gorsuch and Tho Powell to "our Loving friend Edward Roe to ack. above sale. Dated "27th 12th month 1664"
Wit. Tho Gaines   signed Rich Gorsuch
     Howell Powell   Tho Powell
            Rec. 13th Sept.1665.

p. 325. Indenture. 12 Sept. 1665, betw. Hugh Brent of the Co. of Lanc., planter, of one part and Tobias Horton of the same Co.,planter, of the other part. Whereas 200 acres of land lying at the mouth of Haddaway Creek in ffleets bay on the No.side of the sd creek and on the So. side of Corotoman Creek x x was jointly purchased by Brent and Horton from Abya Bonnison of the same Co., planter. This land to be worked in co-partnership during the lives of Brent and Horton.
Wit. Tho Madestard   signed Tobyas Horton
     Rich Marshall   Rec. 1st Oct. 1665.

p. 326. Robert Pollard of Lanc. sells to John Starkey and Hen Pulman of the same Co., plantors, certain land. Dated 2nd Feb 1663/4.
Wit. George - - -   signed Robt Pollard
     Jo Boseman   Mary Pollard
            Rec. 1st Dec. 1665.

p. 327. Thos Powell, senr., of Lanc., for "natural love and affection woh I bear unto Tho Powell my son" gives him 6 cows. Dated 16th Oct.1665.
Wit. Edward Dale   signed Tho Powell
     Katherine Vaughan
"Memo that I Jane the now wife of the within named Tho Powell senr" consents to gift. Dated 16th Oct. 1665.
Wit. Jo Barry (?)   signed Jane Powell
     Rich Syms
            Recorded 1st Dec. 1665.

p. 327. Power of Atty. Will Ironmonger, planter, in the County of
Gloucester to"my wel beloved friend Jo Meredith shipwright in the County
of Lancaster" to make final agreement with Walter Herd regarding a plantation sold him. Dated 22nd March 1665. (sic)
Wit. Jo Walker   signed Will Ironmonger
      Tho Delahay   Rec. 8th Nov. 1665.

p. 328. Ellinor Browne agrees to serve Rich Hale, gent., for two years.
Mr. Hale agreeing to free her from Mr. Boswell. Dated 24th Oct.1665.
Wit. Hum Clerke   signed Ellinor Browne
      Harman ffowkes   Recorded 1st Dec. 1665.

p. 328. Minor Doodes of Lanc., marrynor, "with the consent of Mary my
wife" sells to Peter Montague 200 acres, patented 28th Nov.1654, by James
Gates and by him sold to Minor Doodes. Dated - - Nov. 1665.
Wit. Abraham Davys   signed Minor Doodes
      Tho Pullen   Mary Doodes
                                      Recognit in Cur Co Lanor 8 die Nov 1665
                                      Recorded 1st Dec. 1665.
p. 329. Power of Atty. Minor Doodes to "Lov friend Jo Wells" to ack. sale
of above 200 acres. Dated 7th Nov. 1665.
Wit. Abraham Davys   signed Mary Doodes (sic)
      Peter Montague   Recorded 8th Nov. 1665.

p. 329. Grant. Sir Wm. Berkeley, Knt., to Mr. Jo Edwards, 530 acres adj.
land of Hen Lee. This land formerly granted Geo. Taylor 5th Sept.1650 and
by him deserted. Now regranted and due for transpt. of 11 persons, names
not shown on record, into the colony. Dated at James Citty 22 Mar.1664/5.
                                      signed Will Berkeley
                            Rec. 16 Oct.1665.
                         "Teste Phil Ludwell Cl"
p. 330. John Edwards, Chirurgeon, assigns title to above to Mr. Will
Clappam, senr., 7th Nov. 1665.   signed Jo Edwards
Wit. ThoEllys   Eliz Edwards
      Leo Cacott
Power of Atty. Eliz Edwards to "My Lov friend Mr Edward Dale" to confirm
sale. Dated 7th Nov. 1665.   signed Eliz Edwards
Wit. Tho Ellys
      Leo Cacott   Rec. 1st Dec.1665

Note: I am not altogether certain as to the name shown above as Cacott,
it is quite possible that the name may be Caroll. B.F.

p. 330. Grant. Sr Will Berkeley, knt., to Mr. Davyd ffox, 118 acres,adj.
land belonging to Capt. Hacket. This land formerly granted to Jo Edwards,
chirurgeon, last day of May 1657, and by him deserted. Dated James Citty,
14th Oct. 1665.   signed Will Berkeley.
                                Recorded 16th Oct. 1665.
                                "Test Phil Ludwell Cl"

p. 331. Davyd Fox of Lanc., gent., sells to Jo Edwards of Lanc., chirur-
geon, the above land. Anne ffox the wife of the sd Davyd ffox consents.
Dated 7th Nov. 1665.   signed Davyd ffox
Wit. Jo Dawe   Anne ffox
     Davyd ffox junr.

Power of Atty. Davyd ffox of the Co., of Lanc., gent., to "my wel beloved
friend Richard Lawrence of the afsd County, gent" to ack. above sale.
Anne ffox wife of sd Davyd ffox joins in. Dated 7th Nov. 1665.
Wit. John Dawe   signed Dav ffox
    Dav ffox junr   Ann ffox
                          Recorded 1st Dec. 1665.

p. 332. "Know all men by these presents that on this day the 14th of
Decemb: 1665 personally is appeared before me Nicholas Bayard Secretary
of the Citty of New York admitted by the Rt Honble Colo Rich Niclos
Governr unto his Royal Highness the Duke of York of all his territory in
America Mr Jacobus Vis mercht of this Citty wch certifyed and declared
to have assigned ordained constituted and appointed as he doth assign
ordain constitute and appoint by these presents his trusty and welbeloved
friend Mr Dincke Wesselle (sic) also of New York to be his true and Lawful attorney for him and in his name to - - sue for levy require recover
and receive of all and every person and persons in Virginia W'soever and
especially of Mr Augustine Hoormain Cloys de Kuper Michael Poulse Kerry-
man Mindor Doodes Abraham Shears William Coleman and Samuel Ledewick
all living in Virginia all and every such debts sums of money as by bills
bonds and true accounts appeareth to be justly due unto him the sd Jacobus
Vis giving and granting to his sd attorney ful power thought and authority in and about the premises and upon receipt of any of the sd debts or
any part thereof acquittances or other discharges for him and in his name
to do operate and performe as amply and largely in every respect and to
all intents as he himselfe might or could do if he were personally present
- -ifying allowing and holding firm wth power his sd attorney shal lawfully do or cause to be done in or about the execution of the promises
In witnes whereof he hath hereunto set his hand and seale in New York the
day and year above said"   Signed Jacobus Vis (seale)
Test. Allard Anthony
     Peiter Abriosse   Attested per me
                             Nic Bayard Sec

                    Recorded 11th April 1666.

p. 333. Peter Montague of Lanc., planter, leases to Monor Doodes land
for 54 years. This land having been patented 28th Dec. 1654 by James
Gates, by him sold to Minor Doodes and by him sold to Peter Montague.
Dated 20th Nov. 1665.   signed Pet Montague
Wit. Rich Cooke
      Will Thompson   Rec. 1st Apl.1665.

p. 334. George Vezey of Lanc., assigns to Nathaniel Browne right in
patent to follow and appoints Stephen Tomlin to ack. in Court. Dated 25th
Feb. 1665/6.   signed George Vezey
Wit. John Curtys
      Geo Gilliam
"At Court Co Lanc 14th March 1665."
"Joane Vezey the Widd and relict of the above named Geo Vozey doth freely
consent to the assignment above sd"

        Grant. Sr Will Berkeley, Knt., to George Vezey and Nathaniel Browne
250 acres "bounding S. on the land of Mr Tho Powell x x originally granted to sd Vezey and Browne 5th June 1657 and now renewed". Dated James
Citty, 10th March 1662/3.   signed Will Berkeley
                                          Tho Ludwell Sec
Recognit 14 Mar 1665 per - -Step - Tomlyn and Joane Vezey. Rec.1 Apl 1665.

p. 335. Jo Curtys of Lanc., gentleman, sells to Tho Williams of Lanc.,
planter, 50 acres adj. land of Jo Wortham and the land of Abraham Moone,
decd., etc. Dated 13th March 1665/6.   signed Jo Curtys
Wit. Cuth Potter
     Ra Travers
Power of Atty. Anne Curtys to Mr. Ed. Dale giving consent to sale of 400
acres to Nath. Browne and 50 acres to Tho Willyams. Dated 14 March 1665/6.
Wit. Davyd Allyson   signed anne Curtys
     Robt Beverley   Recorded 1st April 1665.

Note: There seems to be some confusion in regard to the above dates. The
year is prob. 1664/5. B.F.

p. 335. Will Ironmonger "of the County of Gloster planter" sells to
Walter Herd of Lanc., planter, 300 acres, being plantation where Willm
Ironmonger lately lived. Dated 1 Jan 1665   signed Wm Ironmonger
Wit. Tho Dellahay
      Edward Dale   Rec. 1st Apl.1665.
Power of Atty. William Ironmonger to Jo Meredith to ack sale to Davyd
Myles and Walter Herd. Two several conveyances. Dated 10th Feb .1665 (sic)
Wit. Tho Dellahay   signed Wm Ironmonger
     Edward Dale   Rec. 14th March 1665 (sic).

p. 336. Will Ironmonger gives to "my god daughter Ann the daughter of Jo Meredith" a heifer running on the land of Wm Hutchins in Corotoman River, and authorizes "my Lov friend Walter Herd" to ack this deed in Co. Court of Lancaster. Dated 10th Feb. 1665 (sic)

Wit. John Meredith   signed Wm Ironmonger
      Edward Dale   Rec. 1st April 1665 (sic)

p. 337." The deposition of John Troster aged about 36 years sworne saith that being at the house of Minor Doodes in Nansemond the 20th of April 1656 a certain person named Cornelius Powell did request this deponent to write for him a certain note for Minor Doodes to set his hand to so this deponent did vizt I Minor Doodes do promise faithfully to Cornelius Powells that whensoever he departeth out of this county wth his wife and family that I will not sel Degoe the negro servant wch I bought of him no longer then for ten years witnes my hand April the 25th 1656

Witness Tho Troster   Mindor Doodes
      Ja- Abraham

    And the true intent and meaning of the sd note is that Minor Doodes bought Degoe the negro of Cornelius Powell for a slave forever unles Minor Doodes went out of the County wth his wife and family and then if Minor Doodes should sell Degoe the negro he promised he would not sel him for longer time than for ten years and further saith not

      Sworn on the 5th day of March 1665
Before me   Charles Calvert   Jo Troster "
          Recorded 14th March 1665.

p. 337. Power of Atty. Abia Bonnison of ffleets Bay in the County of Lancaster, planter, to "my friend Hugh Brent of the same County, planter" to collect debts. Dated 21st March 1665. (sic)

Wit. Tho Madestard   signed Abya Bonnison
      Rich Stockdale

      Recorded 14th March 1665 (sic)

p. 338. Richard Merryman of Lanc. planter, sells to Will Hall of London, marrynor, 1000 acres for 10.000 lb tobo. Dated 1st Jan. 1665.

Wit. Jo Dawe   signed Rich Merryman
      Dan Harrison   Recorded 1st Apl. 1665 (sic).
" Daniel Harrison

      These are to desire and authorize you x x to ack x x my consent to the sale of 1000 acres of Land made by my husband Rich Merryman unto Mr Will Hall of London marrynor " Dated 13th March 1665.

Wit. Tho Chatwyn   signed Susan Merryman
      Edward Stevens   Recorded 1st Apl 1665.

p. 340. Jarrat Reynolds in Corotoman, milwright, sells to Will Wroughton of Lanc., 200 acres adj. land of Edmond Connoway (sic) being part of 400 acres taken up by Will Neasum and Jarrat Reynolds. The sd Jarret and his wife to ack. this at next Court. Dated 2 Sept 1665 (sic).

Wit. Tho Williamson   signed Jarrat Reynolds
      Marke Ponsax

      Recorded 1st Apl 1665 (sic)

p. 340. James Markmun sells to John Brady 4 head of cattle. Dated 15th
Dec. 1665.   signed Ja Markmun
Wit. Rich Robinson
      Tho Hutton   Rec. 1st Apl 1665(sic)

p. 340. Jo Brady assigns ~~e head of~~ cattle to Tho Markmun son of James
Markmun. One cow to Mary Markmun and one cow to Eliza Markmun the children
of the sd Markmun. Dated 5 Jan 1665 (sic) signed Jo Brady
Wit. Rich Robinson
      Cuth Potter   Rec. 1st Apl. 1665 (sic).

p. 341. 'According to an order of Court the land is divided "betwoixt
Mr Hump Jones and Mr Smiths orphans the sd Jones having the upper part of
the divident being a hundred and fifty acres and the lower part belonging
to the aforesd orphans being 150 acres a line of marked trees according
to bil of sale - - the whole divident surveyed the 26th of March 1664/5"
                        signed Tho Chetwode
                   Recorded 14th March 1665.

p. 341. Grant. Sr Will Berkeley Knt to Will Wroughton, 400 acres bound-
ing upon the Court house land and upon the land of Will White and that of
Jo Merryman. Also upon the land of Mr Neasum, Michl Arme, Daniel Harrys
and of Rich Merryman. North upon the land of Doctor Edwards and that of
Tho Marshal. S.E. upon the land of Jo Nicolls, Will Abby, Mr Lonhill,
Mr. Ball and upon a former "divident of the sd Wroughton." Dated at"Ja
Citty 18 of 7th 1665."   signed Wm Berkeley
              "Recorded 19th 7 1665 Phil Ludwell Cl"

p. 341. Will Wroughton of Lanc., planter, sells land to James James of
Lanc., carpenter. Dated 11th April 1666.
Wit. Tho Daniell   signed Will Wroughton
      Rich Marshall   Rec. 11th April 1666.

p. 342. Thos Bourne of the County of Stafford in Virginia sells to Jo
Bell and Anth Crispe, both of the County of Lanc., a tract of land lying
upon the Pieankitank River, etc. Dated 13th Nov. 1665.
Wit. Will Poole   signed Tho Bourne
      Rich Wadding   Rec. 11 April 1666.
Power of Atty. Thos Bourne to "my beloved friend Geo Wadding" to deliver
bill of sale to the Court. Dated 13th Nov. 1665.
Wit. Will Poole   signed Tho Bourne
      Rich Wadding   Recorded 11 Apl. 1666.

p. 343. Alex Reade of Corotoman in the County of Lanc., sells to Tho
Younge of ffleets bay in the Co., of Lanc., 200 acres from a tract of
300 adj. land of Wm Hutchins and that of Mr. Robt Jones. Dat. 10 Apl.1666.
Wit. Tobyas Horton   signed Alex Reade
     Tho Williamson   Lydia Reade
                              Rec. 11th April 1666.
Power of Atty. Lydia Reade to Tobyas Horton to ack. above sale. Dated 10
April 1666.   signed Lydia Reade
Wit. Tho Williamson
     H. Pine   Rec. 11th Apl.1666.

p. 344." Wm Ironmonger of County of Gloster planter" sells to Davyd Miles
of Lanc., planter, certain land, excepting a reservation for Walter Herd
of one plantation of 300 acres. Dated 8th Jan 1665/6.
Wit. John Meredith   signed Will Ironmonger
     Tho Nash   Recorded 20th Apl. 1666.

p. 345. Sr. Gray Skipwith sells to Mary Bayley "orphan unto Robt Bayley
decd" one brown cow. Dated 9th April 1664.
Wit. Anth Owon   signed Gray Skipwith
     Virgin Giles

          Gray Skipwith , Barrt., sells to Mary Bayley daughter to Robt
Bayley, decd., two milch cows known by the names of Highhorn and Coom.
Dated 16th March 1662.   signed Gray Skipwith
Wit. Cuth Potter
     Giles Cale

"Brother Dale
     Pray do me the favor to acknowledge in Court on my behalfe two bils
of sale for cattle made to Mary Bayley and this my note shal impower you
for the doing of it as ful as any Letter of Attorney
     Sr I have not also only our love presented to yr selfe and my
sister   Sr I am your lo brother
                                 Gray Skipwith
ffebr: primo 1664   "
                              Recorded 11th Apl. 1666.

p. 346. Arthur Nash sells to Mary Bayley daughter unto Robt Bayley,decd.,
one milch cow known by the name of Honesty. Dated 12th Sept. 1664.
Wit. Nick Mason   signed Arthur Nash
     Jo Bristow
Power of Atty. Arthur Nash to "my wel beloved friend Mr Edward Dale" to
ack. above bill of sale. Dated 14th Jan 1664/5.
Wit. Willm Edenden   signed Arthur Nash
     John Gardner
                              Recorded 11th April 1666.

p. 347. Rich Merryman sells to Abrah Bush 200 acres during his natural life and after the decease of the sd Abra Bush unto Daniel son of the sd Abra. Dated 25th July 1663.   signed Rich Merryman
Wit. Edward Dale
      Diana Dale
"Dear Harrison
          These are to desire and authorize you for me in my behalf to acknowledge at the next Court held for the County of Lanc. my free and absolute consent to the sale of 200 acres of land made by my husband Rich Merryman unto Abraham Bush in the behalf of his son Daniel Bush x x x 2nd day of May 1666 "   signed Susannah Merryman
Wit. Michl Arme
      Jo Boring   Recorded 1st Jun 1666 .

p. 348. Hum Jones gives to Elleanor Owen, daughter of Hum Owen, decd., one heifor. Dated 7th May 1666.   signed Hum Jones
No witnesses shown
                          Recorded 9th May 1666.

p. 348. "The 8th of Decemb 1662 "   Augustine Moore, of the old Poquoson in the County of Eliz. Citty in Virginia, with the consent of "my wife Mary Moore" sells to Jo Scarbororo planter, 300 acres on Pieankitank river, granted to sd Moore.
Wit. Will Stokes   signed Augustine Moore
      Tho Stanele   Mary Moore

Power of Atty. Augustine Moore to John Goare to ack. in Court the sale of the above land. Dated 29th Nov. 1665. signed Augustine Moore
Wit. Rich Rante
      Adam Taylor   Recorded 1 June 1666.

p. 349. Edw. Lunsford of Lanc., planter, sells to Jos. Pye of the same Co., planter, 175 acres being part of 350 acres sold Lunsford by Robt. Swan, bordering land of Elias Edmonds. Dated 10th Oct.1665.
Wit. Tho Kendall   signed Edw Lunsford
      Edward Dale

Power of Atty. Edward Lunsford to Mr. George fflower to ack. above sale in Court. Dated 9th May 1666.   signed Edward Lunsford
Wit. Jarratt Reynolds
      Mary fflower
"Mr Therryott I desire you to acknowledge this on my behalfe at the next Court witnes my hand this 10th of Octo 1665"
                          signed Anne Lunsford

                     Recorded 1st June 1666.

p. 350.   Henry Corbyn of the County of Lanc., in Rappa. River in Virga
Esq., sells to George Nicols and Mathew Wilcocke of great Wicoocomooo in
The County of Northumberland, planters, 4000 granted 1st Aug. 1662 to
Corbyn. Dated 10th April 1666.   signed Hen Corbyn
Wit.   Will Ball
         Rich Robinson   Rec, 1 June 1666.
" x x Mrs Alice the wife of Hen Corbyn Esq within named being examined
apart doth fully consent to the sale" of the 4000 Acres. Dat,9 May 1666.
                                 signed Alice Corbin
                             Rec. 1st April 1666 (sic)

         Grant from ffrancys Morryson to Hen Corbyn, gent., 4000 acres in
Rappa. adj. land of Mr Sam Griffin, etc. Dated James Citty, 8 Aug. 1662.
                                 signed   ffr Morryson
                                           Tho Ludwell Sec
28th 7 mo 1664. "Ordered that Hen Corbyn Esq have seven years further time
for seating the land formerly granted (is expired by this patent for seat*
ing)   By the Governors order
                                 ffran Kirkman "

p. 353.   Edmond Micklebororo of the County of Lanc. in Virga., planter,
sells to Moses Buffery of the same Co., planter, 50 acres, for five pounds
Storl. Dated 1st Nov. 1665.   signed Edmond Mickleborow
Wit.   Tho Jones
         Robt Chowning   Rec. 1st Aug. 1666.

p. 354.   "Memorand that I Eliz the wife of Moses Buffery do freely consent
to the sale of 200 acres made by my husband unto Edward Micklebororo woh
land is now in the possession of the sd Micklebororo Witnes my hand this
11th of July 1666"   signed Eliz Buffery
Wit.   Walter Hord
         Edward Dale   Rec. 1st Aug. 1666.

p. 355.   Cuth Potter of the Co. of Lanc., mercht., sells Alex Smith of
Lanc., planter, 700 acres "Beginning at a marked white oak standing by
Mattapony path near the plantation of John Smith x x" Dat 8 Mar 1665/6.
Wit.   Rich Robinson   signed Cuth Potter
         Wm Gordowne   Rec. 11th July 1666.

p. 355.   Will Clappam releases Walter Herd from debt of 500 lb tobo, all
other debts, etc. Dated 7th July 1666.
Wit.   Tho Wharton   signed Will Clappam
         John Meredith
                             Rec. 1st Aug. 1666.

p. 356. Nich Cooke, overseer of the Estate of Hum Owen, decd., in behalf
of the child of the sd Hum Owen, having stated all accounts and received
full satisfaction of Hum Jones, "do fully and absolutely aquit x x the sd
Hum Jones x x from all manner of claims x x concerning the estate of the
sd child until the 13th day of ffebuary Anno Dom 1664 as witnes my hand
this 26th of April 1666 " (sic)   signed Nich Cooke
Wit. Hen Corbyn
      John ffredsham   Rec. 9th May 1666.

p. 356. "Know all men by these presents that I Rich Loes (LOES) and Nich
Cooke in the behalf of the orphts of Olliver Segar do acquit and discharge
Hum Jones Exor to the estate of Hum Owen from all accounts debts of tobo
cattle or hoggs due or belonging to the sd orpht (sic) from the beginning
of the world to the date hereof as witnes our hands this 13th of ffebr
1664"   signed Rich Loes   (LOES)
Wit. Tho Chowning   Nich Cooke
      Arthur Kelly   Rec. 9th May 1666.

p. 356. John Meredith of the County of Lancaster, shipwright to Rich
Peirce of Northumberland, carpenter. - - July 1666.
        WWhereas the above named Rich Peirce and Grace his wife are by
a mutual consent and agreement resolved to sep'te each from other and not
to own each other as man and wife now the condition of this obligation is
such that if the sd Grace shal not own nor challenge the sd Rich as her
husband at any time hereafter neither challenge any parte or parcel of
the estate of the sd Rich either real or personal by the way of thirds or
otherwise and shal also from time to time and at all times for ever hereafter acquit and discharge the sd Rich his Exors and Admrs from the keep-
ing of the two children she now hath and from all trouble wch may happen
to arise or come thereby that this present obligation to be void and of
none effect otherwise to remain and to be in force and virtue
        Hereafter interlined before delivery "
"Sealed and Delivered   signed Jo Meredith
in the presence of
Will Smith
Edward Dale"   Recorded 1st August 1666.

P. 357. Power of Atty. Ruth Eldred, widow and Admr. of the goods and
chattels of Wm Eldred, late marryner and commander of "the ship house of
friendship" to "my trusty friends Edward Goldstone marryner and master of
the ship Susan and Will Hall marryner his mate" to collect accounts from
William Ball of Rappa. and others in Virginia. Dated 2nd Aug. 1660.
Witnesses (in London)   signed Ruth Eldred
Wm Bower
Tho Woodward his servt
Edmond Effard
John ffreebody
James Wilson
Edward Boswell

            (see further entries to follow)

p. 358. Power of Atty. Margaret Phillips, Extx of the last will and
testament of Mathow Phillips, marryner, decd., to Edward Goldstone master
of the ship Susan and Will Hall, his mate, jointly, to collect accounts
from William Ball of Rappa. and others in Va. Dated 7th Aug. 1660.
Wit. Wm Bower   signed   Margaret Philips
     Tho Woodward servt
     John ffreebody

P. 359.   " Laws- - in London
Mr Isaac Foxcroft   Sept the 28th 1660
     These are to advise you that we have sent the goods to the inclosed
Invoice by Capt Pensax who did not deal handsomely with us for he went
away and did neither sign to any bills of lading nor chartor - - therefore
you must get them as well as you can I have here inclosed sent the copy
of the Bosons rect and upon that you may demand them My master would
have those tobaccos you sent to be of a good sort x x my master being out
of town I am forced to write to you now But you wil have more at large by
the Boultamore Sr I have not else but am
                                   Your lo friend to command
                                        Tho Munn
This is the key   ffor my Mr John Hatch
of the chest "
                                   Recorded 3rd March 1660.

p. 359. Indenture 20th Dec. 1660. Mr William White clk and Martha his
wife did in their lifetime mortgage unto Mr John Jeffereys and Mr Thomas
Colclough of London, merchants, for the payment of 13900 lb of tobo, a
parcel of land lying in Lanc. County in Virga., on the No. side of Rappa.,
which land was formerly granted to Mr Thos Brice, decd., by patent dated
27th Oct. 1652, on which the sd Brice lived in his lifetime, except such
parts alienated in his lifetime, by sd Brice, to Mr Jo Payne and to Mr
Jo Edwards. The sd land being given to the sd Martha by Mr Tho Brice, her
former husband, in his last will and testament. And whereas the sd Martha
dying in widdowhood, did in her last will and testament, give the sd land
unto the son and daughter of the sd Will White, decd., and whereas upon
nonpayment of the sd tobo, it was ordered at a Quarter Court of the Governor and Council, March 17 1658, that after notice given unto Mr
Jeremiah White and Mr George Hewet, guardians of the sd children, if they
refused to pay the sd tobo, that the land should be sold for payment.
     And whereas Mr John Jeffereys and Mr Thos Colclough and Mr Jeremiah
White and Mr Geo Hewet, guardians of the sd children, have by a joint
letter of attorney, authorized Colo John Carter, of Lanc. in Va., to make
sale of the sd land, for payment of the debt and the over plus for the
orphans,   Now Col. Jno. Carter sells the land to Colo Edward Carter, of
the County of Nansemun in Virginia, for 330 pounds Sterl. to be paid
according to a bond bearing date of this Indenture.
Wit. Simon Kirby   signed   John Carter
     John Carter jun
     Dan Heast
     Jo Mott   Recorded 1st Feb. 1660/1.

p. 361. Letter of Atty. Dated London, Dec. 29th 1659. "Whereas we understand by an order of the Court held at James Citty the 13th of March 1658 as also from a letter from yourself that Mr Will White and Mrs Martha his wife are both dead and that the sd Martha gave her whole estate unto her husbands children here in England x x" Col. Carter is greatly complimented upon his care of the estate and instructed to sell it to the best advantage.   signed "Sr your Humble Servts
John Jeffryes
Tho Cololough
Jeremiah White) Guardians to Mr
George Hewet) Whites children"

"Subscription
ffor our Honord ffriend
Colo John Carter
in Rappahannock Virga.
   These
per Jo Whittey "   Recorded 9th January 1660/1.

p. 362. Grant. Samuel Mathews, Esq., to Edwyn Connoway, gent., 2500 acres adj. land of John Meredith, etc. Dated at James Citty "last of October 1657"   signed Samuel Mathews
                      W Claybourne Sec
Edwin Connoway of Lanc., gent., sells to Sam Pensax of London, marryner, the above land, excepting 200 acres sold to Will Gordon. Dated 9th Jan. 1660/1.   signed Edwyn Connoway
Wit. John Suart
      Edward Dale   Recorded 1st Feb 1660/1.

p. 363. "Rowland Haddaway aged 45 years or thereabouts sworne x x saieth
that about nine years since going in company with Thomas Gaskins Richard
Budd Abraham Moone and John Dennys our desire was to take up land in
ffleets bay and we went into Corotoman Creek where we looked upon land
and took up some afterwards going into a creek where Hugh Brent now liveth
we gave it the name of Haddaways Creek and I this depont did take up the
land that Hugh Brent now lives upon there being three Indian Cabbins
upon the sd land going over a run above the sd Hugh Brents house we coming
upon the land upon the sd run Abraham Moone asked Thomas Gaskins whether
he liked the sd land or would have any of the same the sd Gaskins answered
no for he thought it would drowne the sd Moone answered if you wil not I
wil have it myselfe the sd Moone likewise took a book out of his pocket
and did set down the bounds of the sd land and further saith not
25 Jan 1659 "   signed Row Haddaway
"Test me Edw Dale Cl Cur"

                              Recorded 1 ffebru 1659 (1659/60)

p. 363. "Assigned by me Colo Henry ffleet unto Everd Peterson all my
right and title of a servt mayd named Margaret Stanley who has to serve
after the date hereof about eight years wch term of servitude I do
warrant to the sd Ever Peterson casualty and death excepted as witnes
my hand the 24th Octob 1659"   signed Hen ffleete
Wit. Simon Overzee

                              Recorded 1 ffeb 1659 (1659/60)

p. 363. Willm Thatcher of Lanc., planter sells to Ebby Bonnison of Lanc.,
planter, 200 acres, formerly belonging to Willm Shirts. Dat. 25 Nov.1659.
Wit. Hugh Brent   signed Will Thatcher
     Hugh Jordan   Rec. 1st Feb. 1659/60.

p. 364.   Whereas there was a judgmt confessed in the Court for the County
of Lancaster, by Tobyas Horton upon 600 acres of land, lying upon the N.
side of ffleets bay in Haddaways creek, to Tho Humphreys, cooper, for the
security of 2 men servts. and 2000 lb of tobo, and whereas Will Clappam,
junr., did pay 1000 lb of tobo and "wil cause satisfaction to be ack upon
record by me the sd Tho Humphrey this present Wednesday the 25th of this
Instant January 1659."
     "Therefore x x I Tho Humphreys coopr for the aforesaid and for
one other 1000 lb of tobo formerly recd of Tobyas Horton have x x x sold
x x to Tobias Horton all that dividet of land containing 600 acres x x"
Dated 25th Jan 1659/60.   signed Tho Humphrey
Wit. Hugh Kinsey
     John Lampart
     Tho Hunter   Rec 1st Feb. 1659/60

                    (see following entry)

p. 364 continued. Whereas there was a judgement confessed in the Court
of Lancaster by Tobias Horton upon 600 acres to Thomas Humphrey cooper
for the security of 2 men servants and 2000 lb of tobo and whereas Will
Clappam Junr did pay the sd x x tobo x x and whereas the sd Tobias Horton
x x had x x agreed with the said Will Clappam Junr x x but this was
obstructed by the sickness and death of the sd William therefore know all
men x x that I Tobias Horton x x for a valuable consideration vizt one
able man and 400 lb of tobo received from the sd Willm Clappam lately
decd have x x sold x x to Willm Clappam son of the sd Willm decd 200
acres of land x x beyond the plantation of Rich Hurrall" Dated 25th Jan.
1659/60.   signed Tobias Horton
Signed sealed and Delivered to Thomas Hunter for the sole use and behoof
of the within named Will Clappam son of Will Clappam decd.
Wit. John Lampart
      Daniel Brerden
      J Huntley
"I Eliz the wife of the aforsd Toby Horton do likewise consent to the sale
of the land" Dated 25th Jan. 1659/60.
                            signed Eliz Horton
                        Recorded 1st March 1659/60.

p.366. Wm Frizell assigns all right to within mentioned bill of sale
"from me to Rowland Mackrowry". Dated 8th Oct. 1659.
Wit. John Lampart   signed Will ffrizell
      Will Daniell
"Recognit in cur 25 Jan 1659 per Ja Mackmun att to ffrizell"
                        Recorded 1st March 1659/60.
Power of Atty. Will ffrizell to James Markmun to answer suit, etc.
Dated 23rd Jan 1659/60.   signed Will ffrizell
                        Recorded 25th Jan. 1659/60

p. 367. Will Thatcher sells 200 acres late in his own occupation to
Arthur Clarke. Dated 20th Jan. 1659/60.
Wit. Ja Bidlecom   signed Will Thatcher
      Geo Veazey   Recorded 1st March 1659/60.

p. 367. John Hohsey of the Citty of Bristol, mercht., agrees to pay to
George Vezey and Nathaniel Brown, one lusty man negro betw the age of 16
and 25, the sd negro to be delivered in the river of Rappa. Dated 1st
Dec. 1659.   signed Jo Hohsey
Wit. Raleigh Travers
      Will Travers
      Jo Simpson   Recorded 25th Jan 1659/60

p. 268. Power of Atty. George Reynolds to "my wel beloved friend Mr
Cuthbert Potter" to demand 1100 lb tobo from Tho Hayward. Dated 22nd Sept.
1659.   signed Geo Reynolds
Wit. Tho Chetwode
      Rich Cheburley   Recorded 25th Jan. 1659/60.

p. 368. Grant Sam Mathews, Esq., to Gervayse Dodson 2000 acres in Potomac ffreshes, above Capt. Brent's, adj. land of Mr. Burbadge and that of Mr. Henry Vincent, for transportation of 40 persons, names not shown in record, into the colony. Dated 27th Aug. 1658.

signed Samuel Mathews
W Claybourne Sec

Rec. 1st March 1659/60.

p. 369. Gorvayse Dodson assigns right in above to Hen Corbyn, gent. Dated 22 Oct. 1659.   signed Ger Dodson
Wit. Will Ayliffe
      Tho Middleton   Rec. 1st March 1659/60
"Whereas the land x x doth properly belong to me John Wood x I x x for a valuable consideration x x sell sd land x x to Henry Corbyn gent."
Dated 1st Nov. 1659.   signed John Wood
Wit. Mary Butcher
      Mary Basnet   Rec. 1st March 1659/60.

Power of Atty. Gorvayse and Isaboll Dodson to Mr M athew Kemp to ack assignment of patent bearing date 27th Aug.1658 for 2000 a tò Mr Henry Corbyn. Dated 22nd Oct. 1659.   signed Ger Dodson
Wit. Will Ayliffe   Isabel Dodson
      Robt Middleton   Rec. 25th Jan. 1659/60

p. 370. Power of Atty. John Wood to Mathew Kemp as above. Dat. 1 Nov 1659.
Wit. Mary Butcher   signed John Wood
     Mary Basnet   Rec. 25th Jan. 1659/60.

p. 370. "Whereas Mr Henry Corbyn did request me to take up a parcel of land in Potomac river 2000 acres I did accordingly find in Mabescoscars Creek bounding upon Capt Streater or Henry Vincents land wch I gave Mr Gervayse Dodson order to survey for me I being then - - him and he upon my imployment and I did - - to show me the said land but Dodson contrary to Law and equity did survey the sd land for himselfe wch sd land I intended for the only use of the sd Mr Corbyn x x and I do by these presents assign all my right x x to the sd Corbyn x x " Dat. 23 Aug. 1659.
Wit. Robt Middleton   signed John Wood
      Mary Tugwell   Recorded 1st March 1659/60.

p. 371. Grant Edward Digges, Esq., to Peter Rigby and George Keeble 600 acres, opp. land formerly in occupation of Mr Will Hockaday. Dated 8th October 1656.   signed Edward Digges
                                    W Claybourne Secy
Recorded 1st March 1659/60.
Peter Rigby assigns right in above to Will Dudley. Dated 27th July 1659.
Wit. Edward Wyatt   signed Peter Rigby
      Rich Carter   Recorded 1st March 1659/60
"Mr Dale These are to intreat you to ack in Court four several deeds of conveyance of land to Mr Will Dudley x x" Dated 29th Sept.1659.
Wit. Jo Snelling   signed Peter Rigby
      Tho Falkner   Recorded 25th Jan. 1659/60.

p. 372. "Whereas I Peter Rigby of the County of Lancaster x x ack x x that I have taken a bill of Will Dudley of the County of Glouster where he has obliged himself for the payment of two able men servts as by bill x x bearing date July 27th 1659 x x now so it is in case that I the sd Rigby do not insure and save harmless and confirm a parcel of land x unto the sd Dudley x x then the bil above mentioned be void x x witnes as I do give firmly from under my hand wth the consent of my wife Margery Rigby witnes my hand this 27 day of July 1659"

Wit. Edward Wyatt   signed Peter Rigby
     Richard Carter   Recorded 1st March 1659/60

p. 372. Surveyed for Mr Peter Rigby 124 acres adj. land of Geo Keeble. Dated 15 Jan 1657/8.   signed Jo Curtys
         Recorded 1st March 1659/60.

p. 372. Edward Dale of Lanc., gent., sells to Robt Rosse, of same Co., planter, certain cattle. Dated 12th March 1659/60.

Wit. Joshua Calbeck   signed Edward Dale
     Daniel Harrison   Recorded 9th May 1660.

p. 373. William Wraughton, in consideration for certain cattle, sells to Dominicke Theriot 27 acres, adj. land late in ownership of Edward Grymes, decd., and agrees to deliver patent for this land before the 25th of Dec. 1660. Also "myselfe and wife" to ack. same. Dated 6th Oct. 1659.

Wit. Tho Roots   signed Will Wroughton
     Will Ball   Recorded 20th May 1660.

Note: Along with the above entry is that to follow. If there is any connection betw the two, it is not evident to me. B.F.

"Mr Potter In behalf of Sr Henry Chichely doth ack the assignment wthin mentioned was intended to Rich Lewys and that the leaving out his name was meerly a mistake and the sd Lewys having fully satisfyed for the same"
       signed Cuthbert Potter
       Recorded 20th May 1660.

p. 374. " Whereas there was a meeting by the parishoners of Lancaster parish and the parishoners of Picankitank for the final ordering of all differences betwixt the 2 parishes concerning the bounds of the sd parishes should be and extend according to an order of the County Court bearing date 10th day of Sept 1657 Provided the levys due from the Lady Lunsfords plantation and other plantations for thetime past be paid to the use of the sd Lancaster parish and this agreement not to make invalid any order of the Court for the recovery of the sd levys In witnes whereof I Henry Corbin on behalf of the parish of Lancaster set to my hand and seale this 14th of Sept 1659 this agreemt to take place from this day"

Wit. John Colepeper   signed Hen Corbyn
     John Rynes   Cuth Potter
       Recorded 20th May 1660.

p. 374. Grant Sir Willm Berkeley to Sam Tucker, 50 acres of land in the County of York, butting upon Cheesmans Creek, adj. land of Thomas Attoway etc. Dated James Citty 2nd June 1643. signed Willm Berkeley
Recorded 20th May 1660.

Samuel Tucker assigns right in above patent to James Williams. Dated 19th
January 1657/8   signed Sam Tucker
Wit. John Wood
      Henry Webb   Recorded 20th May 1660.

p. 374. Mathew Kemp of Lanc., gent., sells to Henry Corbyn of Lanc., gent., 700 acres or last in occupation of one Will Clappam, junr. "the sd Math Kemp for himself and Mrs Dorothy his wife." Dated 20th Nov.1658.
Wit. Myles Dixon   signed Math Kemp
      Cha Norwood   Recorded 20th May 1660.

p. 376. Power of Atty. Benjamin Whiscombe of London, marryner, to Tho Patteson, of the County of Lanc. in Virginia, to collect debts and transact business regarding his plantation. Dated 9th June 1660.
Wit. Edward Dale   signed Ben Whiscom
     Diana Dale   Recorded 11 July 1660.

p. 376. Will Leech, of the Co. of Lanc. in Virginia, planter, sells to Lt Colo Anth Ellyot, 700 acres adj. land of John Benton. Refers to "my now wife Moll Leech" Dated 7th July 1660.
Wit. Math Kemp   signed Will Leech
     Edward Dale   Recorded 20th July 1660.

p. 377. Power of Atty. Thomas Stone and Will Hall, cittizens, mercht and mercht Taylor of London appoint "our trusty and loving friends Mr George Wadding and Mr Francis Gar- - (Garsuch ?) of Pieankitank in Virginia, to collect debts and transact other business. Dated 3rd Jan 1659/60.
Wit. Sam Hopper   signed Will Hall
     Jo Whittey   Tho Stone
     Hen Creyk   Recorded 11th July 1660.

p. 378. Walter Dickenson, late of Corotoman in the Co. of Lanc., sells to Willm Clappam of Corotoman, certain cattle. Dated 9th June 1660.
Wit. James Bidlecom   signed Walter Dickenson
     Tho Powell   Recorded 11th July 1660.

p. 379. "Know all men by these presents that I Sr John Harvey Knt for and in consideration of now almost six months service already past and for his attendance upon me into England in the good ship the Planter of London and after my arrival there to attend me also to the Bath and so to continue with me until the end of November next ensuing paying for his passage forth and back to Virginia and the present gift and delivery of a negro woman servt called ffranke and a youth called ffrancis pepper who hath one year to serve me I say that for and in consideration aforsd and in regard the knowingnes of him Barkum Obert of my dosease and usefulness unto me in respect of my Lameness and not having at this present also or otherwise to gratifye his willingness to do me his best service now in my time of great necessity and suffering I have also given him one milch cow called goulding wch is one of my - - called upon James Island to enjoy forever wth her increase for the relief of his wife who he leaveth in much sorrow for his departure and in case that cow shal by misfortune dye or be lost then I do hereby give and grant unto him or his assgs to make choice of any other out of the stock of cattle belonging unto me in this colony of Virga Dated this 3rd of May 1640"
Wit. Henry ffleete   signed John Harvey

Rec 11 Jul 1660
Edw Dale Cl Cur

Note: In coming upon this unexpected entry in Lancaster County, recorded twenty years after it was dated, I cannot but recall Henry Fleet's misgivings when Sir John had him arrested in Chesapeake Bay some years before and his surprise at the cordial reception given him and the consideration shown by the Governor upon his arrival with his vessels in Jamestown.B.F.

p. 380.   "July 16 1660
Gent   So many and so various have been the complaints to me of and from the Indians of Rappa river that I know not at this distance what judgmt to make of their grievances I do therefore by this writing earnestly desire you to make a diligent enquiry what unnecessary injurys are done to the Indians and how our articles of peace are kept with them and to make a report to me of it against the next Court wch I will show to the Council that will then meet I beseech you to be careful of this for both in humanity and Christianity we ought not to leave them wth out a possibility of subsistance In doing this you wil discharge your duties to God and the country and oblige   Your ffriend and servt
To Collo Carter   William Berkeley
Coll ffauntleroy
Capt Fleete Mr Corbyn
Mr Kempe or any three or four more
that these you shall appoint "   Recorded 12 7th 1660.

(See Sir William's letter to Col. Carter next page.)

116

p. 380.   "Colo Carter
              Since I received your - - from the Commission of what you
did in the business of the Indians I have wth thankfulnes seen an order
of your Court concerning my tobacco and corne so long due that woh I now
desire of you is that you would be pleased to order it to Capt Jennings
for my use
              The Assembly is now shortly to meet where I hope I shall
see you and Mr Corbyn for to that wil I refer the injuryes done to you
and me and if we have not some reparations I shal desire such Public business may be referred to others ffor Gods sake keep the copy of the
commission woh I think did not deserve such language and return as I had
from Colo ffauntleroy The first ship wil bring us joy or sorrow in
extreeme
August the 4th 1660   Your ffriend and Servt
The Subscription thus   William Berkeley
ffor my Honord ffriend
Colo John Carter
          These   "   Recorded 12 7mo 1660.

Note: In regard to language, what about "ffor Gods sake" ? It seems that
Sir William was not altogether without guile- "may be referred to others."
But the good news did come and that changed everything. B.F.

p. 381. Mathew Kemp of Lanc., gent leases to Henry Corbyn of Lanc.,gent.,
700 acres, for 106 pounds, for 99 years. "Mathew Kemp doth for himself &
Dorothy his wife." Dated 12th Sept. 1660.
Wit. Jo Meredith   signed Math Kempe
      Tho Roots
      Tho Bourne   Recorded 12th Sept.1660.

p. 382. Grant. Samuel Mathews, Esq., to John Curtys, 1200 acres for
transportation of 24 persons, names not shown on record, into this
colony. Dated James Citty, 15th March 1657/8.
                               signed Samuel Mathews
                                      W Claybourne Secy
                    Recorded - Sept 1660.
"Jo Curtis and Anne my wife do assign x x our right and title of this
patent unto John Harris x x" Dated 26th Aug. 1660.
Wit. Hen Thacker   signed Jo Curtys
      Tho Oakeley   Anne Curtys
                    Recorded 12th Sept.1660.

p. 383. John Curtys acks. full satisfaction for the 1200 acres above.
Dated 26th Aug. 1660.   signed Jo Curtys
Richard Chomley
Hen Awbrey   Recorded 20th Sept. 1660.

Power of Atty. "John Curtys and Anne Curtys my wife" to "our loving
friend Mr Hen Corbyn" to ack. above sale. Dated 11th Sept. 1660.
Wit. Richard Cholmolay   signed Jo Curtys
      Hen Awbrey   Anne Curtys
                    Recorded 11th Sept. 1660.

p. 383. Grant. Samuel Mathews Esq., to Tho Willys and Robt Middleton 600 acres of land. Dated James Citty 15th Sept. 1658.

signed Samuel Mathews
W Claybourne Secy

Robt Middleton assigns his share of above to Tho Willys. Dat.12 Sep.1660.
Wit. Hen Corbyn   signed Robt Middleton
     John Harris   Recorded 20th Sept. 1660.

p. 384. Power of Atty. "Robert Middleton and Mary Middleton my wife" to John Harrys to ack. above. Dated 12th Sept. 1660.
Wit. Hen Corbyn   signed Robt Middleton
     John Harrys   Mary Butcher (sic)
           Recorded 12th Sept. 1660.

p. 385. Power of Atty. Samuel Weekes of the parish of Pieantk, in the County of Lancaster, appoints "ffrancys my loving wife my true and lawful attorney for me x x"to collect debts due in the Kingdom of England.
Dated 10th Sept. 1660.   signed Samuel Weekes
Wit. Cuth Potter
     Jo Meredith   Recorded 12th Sept. 1660.

p. 385. "Samuel Weekes of the parish of Pieankotank in the County of Lancaster in Virginia shipwright x x for love and affection I bear ffrancys my now loving wife and also for the payment of my debts in England x x sells x x unto Abraham Russel of London mercht all my whole estate x x belonging to me either in England or in Virginia either in my own right or in the right of the aforesaid ffrancys my wife x x"
Dated 10th Sept. 1660.   signed Sam Weekes
Wit. Cuthbert Potter
     Jo Meredith   Recorded 12th Sept. 1660.

Note: This looks to me as though ffrancys were devoid of love and affection for Virginia. There have been others. B.F.

p. 386. Commission of Admr.,according to order of the County Court of Lancaster, upon the estate of James Nicolson, decd., is granted to George Vezey and Nath Brown by the Rt. Honbl. Sr. Willm. Berkeley, Knt., Governr and Capt. General of Virga. Dated at James Citty 20th March 1659/60.

signed Will Berkeley
Recorded 1st April 1660.

Note: The row of impressive titles give no hint of Sir William's uncomfortable position at this moment. B.F.

p. 386. Commission of Admr. upon the estate of Thomas Evans, decd., is granted unto James Gates, according to the order of the County Court of Lancaster, by the Rt. Honble. Sr. Willm. Berkeley, Knt., etc. Dated at James Citty, March 20th 1659/60.   signed Will Berkeley

118

p. 386. Will of Tho Roots. To Mr Thomas Marshall one man servt. named
Willm Stephens, a cow, a gun, etc.
To my Godson, Tho Roten, a "mayd servt named Anne Searne", two
yearling heifers, etc., one half of my pewter, the other half unto my
sister Roten, to be delivered unto my godson and his mother at my decease.
To Samuel Tucker carpenters tools.
To Elizabeth Robinson, two cows to be recorded for the use of
her two children Eliz and Robt Dudley, and one red stuff petticoat and
one white petticoat to the sd Elizabeth.
To my sister Anne White my wife's wearing clothes.
To my godson Tho Edwards, son to John Edwards, Chirurgeon, one
cow. "It is my will and desire that my lov friend Jo Edwards chirurgeon
shal be my full and whole Exor x x I give unto him all the remainder of
my estate x x" Dated 25th Jan. 1660/1.
Wit. John fflower   signed Tho Roots
     Nich George
Prob. by Joh Edwards chirurg 14 Mar 1660.   Recorded 1st Apl 1661.

p. 387. Edward Webb of the County of Lanc., sells to John Colclough 110
acres, which was part of land sd Webb had of Tho Bourne. Dat.2 Mar.1660
Wit. John Bell   signed Edward Webb   (sic)
      John ffisher   Sara Webb
                        Recorded 20 Sep. 1660.

"Aug 27th 1660   Be it remembered that I John Colclough ack. to x x have
sold unto John Needles land within written"
Wit. Willm Evenden   signed John Colclough
     Edward Webb   Mary Colclough
                        Recorded 20th Sept. 1660.

p. 388. John Colclough acks. "all right title of this bil of sale within
written unto John Needles" Dated 19th April 1660. (sic)
Wit. John Bell   signed Jo Colclough
      Anth Crispe   Recorded 20th Sept. 1660.

p. 388. Power of Atty. "To all Xtian Peoples x x know ye that we John
Colclough Painter of the County of Lancaster and the par'sh of Pieankotank
and my wife Mary Colclough do appoint x x my true and wel beloved friend
Mr Tho Bourne planter of the County of Lancaster and of the par'sh of
Pieankitank our attorney x x to acknowledge sale of land to Mr John
Needles x x " Dated 27th Aug. 1660.   signed Jo Colclough
Will Bawdes   Mary Colclough
Will Edendon   Recorded 12th Sept. 1660.

p. 389. Power of Atty. Sarah Webb wife unto Edward Webb, planter, of the
County of Lancaster, of the parish of Pieankitank, "do ordain and appoint
my Honord husband my true and lawful attorney x x to acknowledge sale of
land by him to John Colclough."   signed Sarah Webb
Wit. Willm Edenden
     Anne Nash   Recorded 12th Sept. 1660.

p. 389. Will Wroughton sells to John Bruthet 200 acres being part of 400
acres "formerly surveyed for Rich fflynt and myselfe." Refers to sd John
Brauthet. Dated 27th Sept. 1654.   signed Will Wroughton
Wit. Abra Moone
      Jo Edwards
Jo Brauthet assigns his right in above to Tho Bourne. Dated 12th Sept 1660.
Wit. Tho Roots   signed Jo Branthett
      Daniel Johnson
                          Recorded 20th Sept. 1660.

Note: The spelling of the names above follows the original record. BF.

p. 390. "Gilbert the son of John and Annys Jackson was baptized Novemb
the 6th 1660 and dyed the same night"

p. 390. Power of Atty. John Walker of the County of Rappa taylor to Mr
Tho Chetwode together with Willm Pue to sell to Robt Pritchard 860 acres
in Lancaster belonging to sd Walker and the sd Wm Pue. Dated 16 Nov.1660.
Wit. John Curtys   signed   John Walker
      Edward Dale   Recorded 20th Nov.1660.

p. 390. Power of Atty. John Woodington of "Warrany in the County of New
Kent in Virginia" to Thos Hunter to ack. in Court sale to William
Wroughton of Corotoman of land patented 15th Jan 1658/9. Dated 22nd May
1660.   signed John Woodington
Wit. Robt Osborne
      Richard Spicer   Recorded 14th Nov. 1660.

p. 391. Grant Saml Mathews, Esq., to John Woodington of 27 acres lying
in County of Lancaster, adj. land of Edward Grymes, decd. Dated James
Citty, 15 Jan. 1658/9.   signed   Saml Mathews
                                              W Clauborne Sec
                          Recorded 14th Nov. 1660.

John Woodington assigns right in patent for 27 acres to William Wroughton.
Dated 22 May 1660.   signed   John Woodington
Wit. Reuben Osborne
      Richard Spicer   Recorded 22nd Nov. 1660.

p. 392. Whereas Ebbya Bonnison and Hugh Brent having bought 400 acres betw
them, formerly belonging to Wm Shirts and Wm Lippert, Bonnison and Brent
divide the land, each taking 200 acres. Dated 11th Aug. 1660
Wit. Rich Stanford   signed Abia Bonnison
      Robt Sickes   Hugh Brent
                          Recorded 20th Nov. 1660.

p. 392. Grant. Richard Bennett, Esq., to Thomas Humphrey, 600 acres in Northumberland Co., upon the northward part of ffleets bay, half a mile up Hadaways creek or thereabouts, abuting Easterly upon a branch of the sd creek, N.W. upon another branch of the sd creek, Westerly into the main woods. Dated 1st Sept. 1654. signed Rich Bennet

W Claibourne

Recorded 20th Nov. 1660.

" I do assign and set over unto Tobias Horton and his assgs forever all my right title and interest in this patent witnes my hand this 14th of Nov 1660"   signed   Tho Humphreys

Wit.   Tho Hunter

Thos Madestard   Recorded 20th Nov. 1660.

p. 393.   " I Mary wife of the aforenamed Tho Humphreys do consent to the sale above mentioned witnes my hand " Dated 14th Nov. 1660.

signed   Mary Humphrey.

Recorded 20 Nov. 1660 Edward Dale Cl Cur.

pages 394 to 399 blank.

pages 399 to 460 contain 18th century items.

p. 461.   "A Court held for Lancaster County on Fryday the 13th day of June 1740.

Thomas Edwards Clk of this County producing in Court sundry Loose sheets and Quires of Paper containing the most authentic and ancient records belonging to this County It is the opinion of the Court that the same ought to be fairly transcribed in a bound book for that purpose forthwith to be provided and it is ordered that the sd Thomas Edwards procure the sd book at the charge of this county and that he transcribe the sd records with all convenient speed and It is further ordered that the sd Thomas Edwards be paid for his labour and trouble therein as soon as the whole work that be compleat and carefully examined and alphabetted the sum of two thousand pounds of tobacco to be raised for him in this County Levy

Copia Test   T Edwards Cl Cur

In Pursuant to the above written order the Records in this Book before contained and written Have been carefully transcribed and faithfully compaired examined and alphabetted from the original sheets and Quires wherein the same was and heretofore recorded

by

T Edwards   Cl Cur "

In the use of this index please note that the page numbers shown are those in the original Record Book. And please particularly note that the same name will often appear in two or more entries under the same page number. B.F.

Budd, Jno. 66.
    Rich. 41. 363.
Buer, Wm. 132.
Buffery-see Baffery
Bunbury, Tho. 59. 156. 186.
Burbage, Mr. 368.
    Col. Thomas, 130.
Burch, Geo. 103.
Burford, Wm. Wm.
Burne, Tho. 28.
Burnham, Alice, 46. 51.
    Eleanor, 46.
    Francis, 46.
    John, 46.
    Rowland, 46. 51. 88. 150.
        223. 274.
    Thomas, 46.
Burroughs, John, 54.
    Tho. 94.
Burt, Ann, 15.
Burrill (Burwell ?) Robt. 40.
Bush, Abraham, 324. 347.
    Daniel, 347.
Bushrode, Richd. 321.
    Thos. 19.145.
Butcher, Andrew, 68. 180. 181.
    Mary, 180. 181. 204. 205.
        369. 370. 384.
Butler, Dorothy, 28.
    Franc. 85. 86. 94.
    James, 244.
    Mary. 244.
Butt, James, 10. 28. 91. 136.

Cable, Jno. 15.
Cacott, Leonard, 173. 220. 235.330
Calbeck, Joshua, 372.
Cale, Giles, 263.264.266.297.345.
Calvert, Charles, 337.
Campian, Jno. 309. 310.
Canaway, Jno. 291.
Canille, Wm. 222.
Cano (Cane ?) 245.
Cant, David, 157.
Capell, Wm. of London, 322. 323.
Caplan, Wm. 100. 200.
Carne, Wm. 38.
Carpenter, Fra. 204. 205.
Carroll.-the name shown here as
    Cacott may possibly be Carroll.
Carter, Major, 120.
    Col. Edward, 360.
    Elizabeth, 25.

Carter, Colonel John, 1. 6. 15. 19.
    25. 87. 110. 118. 140.151.
    175. 185. 208. 209. 218.
    233. 234. 299. 360. 361.
    380.
    John, Junior, 360
    Richd. 371. 372.
    Thos. 28. 123. 158. 175. 209.
        272. 283.
Casby, Robt. 323.
Cates, James, 158.
    Sarah, 158.
Catesby, Jane. 293.
Catlet, Jno. 82. 83. 92.
Cely, Thos of London. 77.
Cerliff, Andrew, 38.
Chambers, Robt. 8. 96.
Chamblett, Randolph, 59. 235.
Chamley, Erasmus, 15. 114.
Chandler, Rich. 80.
Charington, Wm.
Charles II, 210.
Chatwyn, Tho. 263.
Chavanne, Peter, 286.
Cheburley, Rich. 368.
Cheeke, Anth. 229. 265.
Chene, Tho. 263.
Chernell, Jos. 276.
Chetwode, Elizabeth, 281. 282.
Chetwode, Thomas, 45. 87. 102. 118.
    146. 147. 154. 163. 169.
    209. 212. 220. 221. 223.
    233. 234. 235. 257. 281.
    283. 296. 298. 300. 302.
    304. 310. 323. 324. 341.
    368. 390.
Chatwyn, Thos. 338.
Chew, Sam. 265.
Chewers, Tho. 87.
Cheyney, Marg. 288.
    Wm. 288.
Chicheley, Sir Henry, 87. 149. 263.
    268. 269. 373.
Chilton, Elizabeth, 273.
    Stephen, 257.
Chinley, Jno. 300.
Chinn, Jno. 239. 240.
Chivers, Tho. 87.
Cholmondeley, Erasmus, 15. 114.
    Richd. 203. 383.
Chonninge, Robt. 141.
Chowne, Tho. 184.
Chowning, Robt. 141. 223. 242. 243.
    267. 294. 314. 353.
    Thomas, 356.

Edwards, Eliz. 373. 330.
    John, 1. 20. 27. 57. 146. 173.
        207. 214. 217. 221. 230.
        235. 236. 272. 273. 317.
        329. 330. 341. 360. 386.
        389.
Edwards, Tho. 386.
Effard, Edmond of London, 357.
Eldred, Ruth, 357.
    Captain William, 357
Elgar, Tho. 77.
Elliott, Mr. 57.
    Lt. Col. Anth. 110. 157. 189.
    226. 376.
Ellis, Lt. Coll. 38.
    Jno. 307.
    Thomas, 330.
Elmore, Peter, 277.
Eltonhead, William, 151.
Emberson, Wm. 277.
English, Jno. 15.
Esterbrook, Jacob, 111.
Etty, Christopher, 299.
Evans, Lawrence, 120.
    Thos. 26. 143. 386.
Evenden (Edenden) Wm. 346. 387. 388.
    389.
Ewery, (Avery ?) Emanuel, 283.

Fabian, Fra. 79.
Fairwaithes & Co. 19.
Falkner, Tho. 371.
Faroe, Edmond, 212. 229. 322. 323.
Farrington, Robt. 255. 297. 298. 300.
Fauntleroy, Capt. 107.
    Col. 363. 389.
    Eliza. 107.
    Moore, 9. 18. 23. 40. 108.
    109. 116. 118. 137. 158.
    263.
Fawdon, Capt. Geo. 255.
Fenwick, Cuth. 149. 151.
    Thos. 151.
Ferman, Nich. 137.
Fish, Jno. of London, 229. 237. 322.
    323.
Fisher, Jno. 229. 387.
    Reuben, 301.
Fleet, Henry, 6. 28. 64. 119. 138. 144.
    171. 173. 263. 264. 363. 379.
    380.
Fleet, John, 145.

Fleming, Alex. 223.
    Walter, 40.
Fletcher, Jno. 224. 227.
Flint, Richd. 389.
Flower, Mr. 298.
    George, 167, 182. 230.
    273. 287. 297. 300.
    317. 349.
Flower, John, 142. 273. 386.
    Mary, 230. 349.
    Richd. 140.
Floyne, Teague, 67. 96. 155.
Forman, Nick. 43.
Forset, Mr. 4.
Fowkes, Mr. 185.
    Harman, 328.
    John, 6.
Fox, Anne, 331.
Fox, David, 6. 127. 137. 148. 198.
    210. 211. 215. 216. 239.
    241. 250. 264. 283. 293
    330. 331
Fox, David, Junior, 331.
    Hannah, 241. 283.
    List of Silver, 241.
    Costumes, 284.
Foxcroft, Mr. 127. 185.
    Isaac, 148. 185. 264.
    265. 359.
Fredsham, Jno. 356.
Freebody, Jno. of London, 357. 358.
Freshwater, Thos. 263.
Friste, Robt. 263.
Frizell, Glasbeck, 131.
    Wm. 38. 127. 168. 169. 366.
Fullerton, Matth. 165.
Fullyham, Anth. 8.
Furman, Rich. 6.

Gaines, Francis, 38.
    Thomas, 324.
Gardowne, Wm. 355.
Garland, Mr. 8.
    Peter, 96. 137. 138.
Garner, Nick. 215.
Garrett, Anne, 33.
    William, 222.
Gaskins, Thos. 312. 363.
Gates, Jas. 143. 158. 165 328. 333.
    386.
Gates, Sarah, 143. 158.
Gatlin, Jno. 15.

Hoy, Wm. 285.
Hubbard, Mr. 52.
    Robt. 255.
Huddle, Edmund, 121.
Hudds (Budd ?) Jno. 66.
Huff, Robt. 320.
Hugh, Richd. 11.
Hugell, Nich. 263.
Hughes, Ed. 15.
Hulett, Lanr. 124.
Hull, Mr. 145.
    Jno. 307.
Humphreys, Jno. 155. 213. 313.
    Mary, 392.
    Matthew, 80. 99.
    Thos. 145. 151. 265. 364.
    392.
Hunt, Jno. 6. 84.
    Joseph, 282.
    Michael, 282.
    Thos. 75.
Hunter, Tho. 75. 364. 390. 392.
Huntley, J. 364.
Hurrall, Rich. 364.
Hurst, Toby, 44. 76.
Husle, Mr. 127.
Hutchins, Chas. 307.
    Eliz. 287. 293.
    Wm. 104. 105. 140. 234.
    254. 267. 283. 287.
    301. 336. 343.
Hutchinson, Wm. 216.

Innerey, Geo. 143.
Ireland, Wm. 102.
Irish, Jno. 27. 28. 63.
Ironmonger, Wm. of Gloucester Co. Va.
    277. 317. 327. 335. 336.
    344.
Ixom, Fredk. of London, 291. 305.

Jackman, Mr. 15. 84.
    Anthony, 99. 311.
Jackson, Annys, 390.
    Gilbert, 390.
    John, 161. 268. 269. 390.
Jadwyn, Jno. 149. 288. 289.
James, Mr. 299.
James, James, 267. 301. 341.
    Richard, 109.
    Thomas, 62. 295.
Janiser, Captain, 304.

Jeffreys, John of London, 46. 122.
    149. 263. 264. 265. 284.
    359. 361.
Jellson, Andrew, 102.
Jenner, Thos. 320.
Jennings, Capt. 274. 380.
    Peter, 208
Jiggles, Thos. 121.
Johnson, Anne, 235.
    Daniel, 59. 128. 136. 194.
    235. 265. 389.
    George, 119.
    Love, 174. 176.
    John, 6. 50. 119.
    John, Junior, 50.
    Peter, 6.
    Reynold, 33. 156.
    Thos. 306.
    Wm. 15. 32. 36. 95. 99.265.
Jollson, Mr. 15.
Jones, Mr. 235.
    Evan, 254.
    Hannah, 158.
    Hum. 258.289.341.348.356.
    John, 20. 21. 33. 77. 158.
    181. 207. 219. 220.
    299. 302.
    Margaret, 159.
    Leonard, 117. 264.
    Rice, 10. 33. 99. 102.176.
    278.
    Robert, 318. 343.
    Thomas, 159. 191. 353.
Jordan, Geo. 19.
    Hugh, 188. 196. 197. 296.
    Robt. 291. 263.
Joyner, Christo. 77.
Juxon, Alice, 121

Kapell, Jno. 15.
Keeble, Geo. 313. 371. 372.
    Margaret, 258.
    Mary, 313.
Kelly, Arthur, 356.
    Roger, 222. 323.
Kemp, Mr. 380.
    Dorothy, 275. 374. 381.
    Edmond (?) 148. 208. 265.
    Edward, 148. 265.
    Eliz. 216. 258.
    Matthew, 64. 127. 148. 171.
    208. 210. 211. 216.
    223. 265. 269. 274.
    275. 369. 370. 374.
    376. 381.

Woodward, Thomas of London, 357. 358.
Workeman, Mark, 321.
Wortham, Jno. 132. 245. 296. 335.
Wright, Arthur, 154.
      Richd. 265.
      Wm. 103. 110. 255.
Wroth, Tho. 232.
Wroughton, Mrs. 373.
      Joan, 192.
      William, 61. 192. 199. 214.
         224. 235. 238. 302. 340.
         341. 373. 389. 390. 391.
Wyatt, Edward, 275. 371. 372.

Yates, James, 18.
Yeo, Capt. Leo, 77.
York, the Duke of, 332.
Young, Christopher, 77.
      John, 109. 116.
      Robert, 15. 28. 99.
      Thomas, 343.
      William, 307.

www.ingramcontent.com/pod-product-compliance
Lightning Source LLC
Chambersburg PA
CBHW021832020426

42334CB00014B/593